the perfect handmade bag

the perfect handmade bag

Recycle and reuse to make 35 beautiful totes, purses, and more

Clare Youngs

CICO BOOKS

LONDON NEW YORK

Published in 2009 by CICO Books

An imprint of Ryland Peters & Small Ltd

20–21 Jockey's Fields

London WC1R 4BW

519 Broadway, 5th Floor

New York, NY 10012

www.cicobooks.com

10 9 8 7 6 5 4 3 2

A CIP catalog record for this book is
available from the Library of Congress
and the British Library.

ISBN-13: 978 1 906525 81 1

Printed in China

Editor:	Alison Wormleighton
Designer:	Barbara Zuñiga
Illustrator:	Kate Simunek
Photographers:	Carolyn Barber and Emma Mitchell
Stylists:	Rose Hammick and Catherine Woram

Disclaimer: CICO Books has made every effort
to provide safe and accurate instructions for
the projects in this book. However, the
publisher cannot accept liability for injuries or
property damage that might occur from
attempting to make the projects.

contents

introduction

Most of us have a selection of purses, totes, and other bags to see us through our busy daily lives. Not only are they a practical means for carting around all those important bits and pieces, but bags are also very much a fashion statement. Any bag you choose to carry reflects your own personal style.

Fashions come and go, with the big design houses changing the look every season. Nowadays even fake designer purses are a multi-million-dollar business. This book shows you how to make a wide range of fashionable bags, from contemporary and capacious weekenders to chic little evening purses and charming children's bucket bags. What's more, they are all made from materials you already have, so they cost next to nothing. Turn a tea towel into a smart tote, or a burlap sack into a stylish and original shoulder bag. In next to no time, you will be able to transform an old blanket, an odd glove, and a few scraps of discarded clothes into a stunning and unique purse.

The projects are great fun and not at all difficult to make. With clear step-by-step instructions, this book will encourage you to experiment and give you the confidence to make practical as well as beautiful bags for yourself, family, and friends.

NOTE: Dimensions always show the width first. Don't mix your measurements—use either inches or metric, but not both, in one project, because the equivalents are not always exact.

sourcing materials

You can make a bag out of practically anything—the opportunities really are endless. While researching this book, I read about one boy who made a backpack out of an old computer with all the insides taken out. You have to give him credit for his inventiveness, but I imagine it was not very practical!

All the bags I have created for this book are made from fabric I've recycled from something else. Clothes and accessories are a prime source. Apart from clothing, consider using any materials you may have lying around the house—from old curtains, tablecloths, and napkins to handkerchiefs, tea towels, even thin rugs and blankets. Keep an eye out at flea markets and thrift shops for purses that you can take apart in order to reuse the handles, interfacing, or buckles.

Before throwing away clothes that are too tired to send to thrift shops, salvage the zippers, buttons, hanging ribbons, lining, and anything else that could be useful one day. Keep broken necklaces and save ribbons from wrapping. Save all your fabric scraps to use for patchwork or labels. An odd glove can provide plenty of fabric for an appliquéd design.

Look in unlikely places for materials. The garage or shed may yield some sheets of plastic or netting. The back of a coat rack may hide scarves that you had forgotten all about. Utilize whatever you find, experiment, and have fun creating. Whatever you come up with, you know you will have something that is original and unique.

purses

wooden-handle purse

Keep an eye out for old wooden-handle purses in thrift shops and garage sales. Although the purse itself might be old and worn, the handles are probably in good shape. Cutting off the old fabric and making a new purse to attach to these handles takes only minutes, and the result looks brand-new and stylish.

MATERIALS

2 pieces of main fabric and 2 pieces of lining fabric, each about 22 x 13in (56 x 33cm)

1 side-seam label (see page 121)

Matching sewing thread

1 pair of wooden handles

1 Using the template on page 122, round off the two bottom corners on each piece of fabric. Place the two main fabric pieces with right sides together. Pin and stitch a ⅝in (1.5cm) seam down both side edges, around the curves, and along the bottom edge, leaving the top 7½in (19cm) of each side edge unstitched. Repeat for the two lining pieces, but leave a 4in (10cm) opening in the seam along the bottom edge. On the lining at the point where the stitching starts at each side edge, clip into the seam allowances for ⅝in (1.5cm).

2 Turn the lining right side out and place it inside the main fabric, with right sides together. Insert a label at one side edge just above the clips, pointing inward; pin. Pin the main-fabric front to the lining front along the unstitched portions of the side edges and across the top edge. Stitch a ⅝in (1.5cm) seam, pivoting at the corners. Repeat for the back of the bag. Pull the main fabric through the opening in the bottom edge of the lining; turn in the edges of the opening, pin, and slipstitch.

3 Tuck the main fabric inside the lining so the lined bag is inside out. Wrap one top edge over one handle, wrong sides together. Pin it in place at least 1in (2.5cm) from the handle, pushing material together as you go to gather it onto the handle. Baste and then stitch, flattening the material as you sew and then bunching up the sewn portion. Hand sew a few stitches at each end, to join the fabric tightly together under the handle, helping it stay in place. Repeat for the other top edge and handle. Turn the bag right side out, and press.

ruffle-top purse

This is a duffel bag with a difference, as the bold ruffles at the top give it a fun, frivolous look. The pretty paisley fabric from a cotton dress is ideal for a summer purse, or you could make a winter version using heavier fabric.

1 Using the template on page 122, round off the lower corners of the front and back pieces. With right sides together, pin the main-fabric front to the back. Stitch a ⅝in (1.5cm) seam down the sides, around the curves and along the bottom, leaving the top 5½in (14cm) unstitched at each side. Clip into the seam allowance 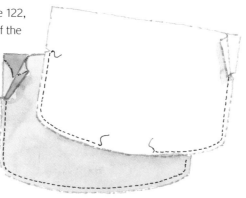 on the curves. Press the seams open. Turn right side out. Repeat for the lining, leaving a 4in (10cm) opening in the seam at the bottom. At the point where the stitching starts and ends, clip into the seam allowances for ⅝in (1.5cm).

MATERIALS

2 pieces of main fabric and 2 pieces of lining fabric, each 24¾ x 17in (63 x 43cm), for front and back

2 pieces of main fabric, each 24¾ x 6½in (63 x 16.5cm), for ruffles

1 side-seam label (see page 121)

2 pieces of main fabric, each 2 x 20in (5 x 51cm), for handles

Matching sewing thread

2 pieces of rubber tube or plastic rope, each ⁵⁄₁₆in (7mm) in diameter and 19¼in (49cm) long

2 Turn under ¼in (5mm) and then a further ⅜in (1cm) along one long edge and both ends of each ruffle. Press, pin, and stitch. With raw edges even, pin one ruffle to the main-fabric front along the top, so the ruffle and the front are both right side up, and the hemmed ends are equidistant from the side edges of the bag. Baste ½in (1.2cm) from the top edge. Repeat to attach the other ruffle to the top edge of the back.

3 Turn the main fabric wrong side out, leaving the lining right side out. Place the lining inside the main fabric, right sides together, with the ruffle sandwiched between them. Pin the lining front to the main-fabric front and the lining back to the main-fabric back along the unstitched parts of the side edges, pushing the ruffle out of the way. Insert a label, pointing inward, at one of these edges. Stitch ⅝in (1.5cm) seams, starting the stitching 1⅜in (3.5cm) from the top seamline and being careful not to stitch through the ruffle. Press the seams open.

4 Pin the lining front to the main-fabric front and the lining back to the main-fabric back along the top edges, turning under the side seam allowances. Stitch ⅝in (1.5cm) seams.

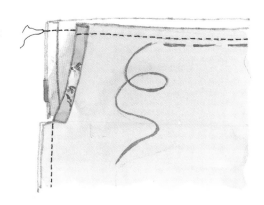

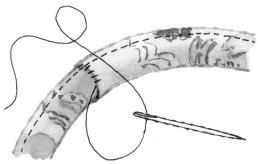

5 Turn the bag right side out through the opening in the lining. Turn in the edges of the opening, pin, and slipstitch it closed. Push the lining down into the bag and press the top edge. On both front and back, pin and topstitch ¾in (2cm) from the top edge and parallel to it, through the main fabric, ruffle, and lining, creating a casing on the front and another on the back.

6 Turn under ⅜in (1cm) on each long edge of one handle, and press. Fold it in half lengthwise, wrong sides together, and press. Pin and stitch close to the long edge. Push one of the lengths of rubber tube or rope through this fabric tube. Repeat for the other handle, and then thread these covered handles through the casings in the bag front and back.

7 To join the two ends of each handle together, turn under the raw edge at one end of the handle and push the other end inside it. Slipstitch the two ends together. Slide the handles around so that the seams are hidden inside the pockets. Hand sew a few stitches just beneath each handle at each side seam to secure.

felt corsage purse

Here's another purse that makes a virtue of necessity. I made it from a cardigan sweater that I felted, but because the wool shrinks so much during the felting process I constructed it from separate panels. Putting the seam allowances for the panels on the outside gives it a very fashionable look and adds to the interest of the design. It is also practical, because felt does not ravel. The corsage, made from the same felted wool, is removable, so you can wear it separately if you wish.

MATERIALS

4 pieces of lining, each 6 x 10in (15 x 26cm)

1 piece of lining, 8 x 4in (20 x 10cm)

1 felted wool sweater (see page 116)

1 side-seam label (see page 121)

Matching sewing thread

2 large safety pins

1 Taper the sides of the four lining pieces so they are 6in (15cm) wide at the top and 4¼in (11.5cm) wide at the bottom, with a depth of 10in (26cm). Using the oval template on page 122, cut out a base from the remaining lining piece. From the sweater, cut four panels and a base to the same size as the lining pieces. Pin the side edges of two wool panels with wrong sides together, and stitch a ¼in (5mm) seam. Repeat to join all four panels at the side edges, inserting a label (pointing outward) in one of the seams. With wrong sides together, pin the panels to the base. Stitch a ¼in (5mm) seam all around. Turn under and press ⅝in (1.5cm) around the top edge. Make the lining in the same way, but join the seams with right sides together.

2 For each of the two handles, cut a double-thickness length along the fold of the sweater ribbing, 1 x 16in (2.5 x 40cm). Pin the two cut edges of one handle together and topstitch close to the edge; repeat for the other handle. Pin the ends of one handle to the inside of the main-fabric front at the top, 2¼in (6cm) from the side seams and with the ends overlapping the top edge by ⅝in (1.5cm); baste. Attach the other handle to the back in the same way. With the main fabric right side out and the lining wrong side out, put the lining inside the main fabric. Aligning the seams, pin the turned-under edges of the main fabric and lining together around the top, sandwiching the handles between them; topstitch ¼in (5mm) from the edge.

3 For the corsage use the petal template on page 122 to cut nine petals from the sweater. Also cut a 4¾ x 1½in (12 x 3.5cm) piece and an 8 x 2in (20 x 5cm) piece from the sweater. Turn these strips into fringes by making parallel cuts in them ⅛–¼in (3–5mm) apart, stopping ⅜in (1cm) from one long edge. Roll up the smaller fringe tightly, hand sewing back and forth across the base as you wind. After you've rolled up the smaller fringe, carry on with the larger fringe, lining up the base edge with that of the smaller fringe and continuing to hand sew across the base as you wind.

4 Sew overlapping petals around the base. Place two safety pins on the base, and secure by hand sewing a small circle of wool over them. Pin the corsage in position on the bag.

variation

Why not experiment with different contrasting fabrics when putting together the corsage—petals of alternate colors will add a pretty effect to the finished bag. Try cutting smaller lengths of material when making the fringes, then cut the same length again in a different color and sew them together before you begin rolling the fringe.

appliqué purse

This purse looks so contemporary and will add a splash of color on a dull winter's day. I have used thick felted wool from a coat, with small scraps of thin felted wool for the machine-appliquéd petals. The beauty of felted wool is that the seams don't fray.

MATERIALS

Scraps of felted wool or fleece in different colors

1 piece of thick felted wool, 12 x 27¼in (31 x 69cm), for front/back

2 pieces of thin felted wool, each 9 x 4in (24 x 10cm), for lining

1 side-seam label (see page 121)

Matching sewing thread, to match scraps as well as bag fabric

1 Using the petal template on page 122, cut out 12 petals from the scraps of thin felted wool or fleece. Arrange the petals on the right side of the top half of the front/back piece. Pin and baste in place, and then topstitch close to the edge.

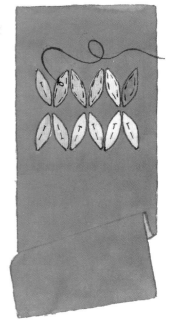

2 With wrong sides together and the top edges even, pin a lining piece to each end of the front/back piece, centering it between the side edges. Baste and then topstitch close to both long edges of the lining. Using the template on page 122, draw the cut-out shape in the center of one piece of lining. Cut out the shape and then topstitch close to the edge of the cut-out. Fold the front/back piece in half crosswise, with wrong sides together and the raw edges even, and draw through the cut-out to mark on the lining where the cut-out should be on the other end. Open out the fabric again, and tidy up the outline using the template. Cut out and topstitch as for the first cut-out.

3 Fold the front/back piece in half crosswise with right sides together and the raw edges even; pin down the sides. Insert a side-seam label, pointing inward, in one seam. Stitch ¼in (5mm) side seams. Turn right side out.

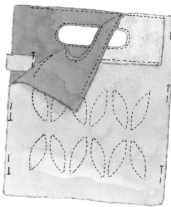

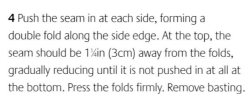

4 Push the seam in at each side, forming a double fold along the side edge. At the top, the seam should be 1¼in (3cm) away from the folds, gradually reducing until it is not pushed in at all at the bottom. Press the folds firmly. Remove basting.

two-tone embroidered purse

For this stylish, understated purse, which is two shades of beige on the front and two shades of gray on the back, I took inspiration from a Japanese design. With the simplest of stitches, such as French knot, you can create wonderful graphic designs. To ring the changes, try other simple shapes (such as a heart, a star, a spiral, or a flower), bright multicolors, different handles, other stitches—the combinations are endless.

MATERIALS

2 pieces of felted wool in different colors and 2 pieces of lining fabric, each 12 x 10¾in (31 x 27.5cm)

Tapestry yarn in shades close to colors of felted wool

1 side-seam label (see page 121)

Scraps of lining fabric, for loops to hold handles (optional)

Matching sewing thread

1 pair of wooden handles with holes in the ends

Fabric marker that will fade away

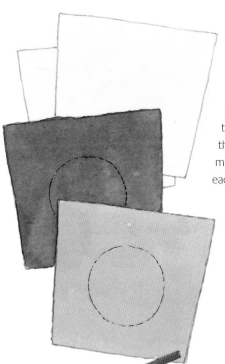

1 Taper the sides of one lining piece so it is 12in (31cm) wide at the top edge and 8¾in (22.5cm) wide at the bottom edge, with a depth of 10¾in (27.5cm). Use this as a pattern to taper the sides of the other lining piece and the two wool pieces. Using the fabric marker, draw a circle in the center of each wool piece. The circles on this bag each have a diameter of 5in (13cm) but you could alter the size.

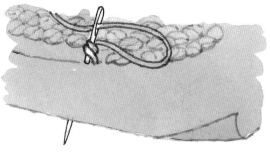

2 Starting in the center of the circle, embroider a French knot. To do this, bring the yarn up through the fabric, leaving a 6in (15cm) tail on the wrong side. Holding the yarn taut between the forefinger and thumb of whichever hand is not holding the needle, twist the pointed end of the needle twice around the yarn. Insert the needle back into the fabric close to where it emerged, and pull the twisted yarn down the needle so it is on the fabric. Push the needle through to the back of the work. Embroider more French knots close to each other, until you have filled the whole circle. To finish off, weave the end of the yarn into the backs of the stitches on the wrong side, and then cut it close to the fabric. Thread the tail that was left at the beginning onto your needle, and work it into the backs of the stitches in the same way.

3 Repeat step 2 on the other piece of felted wool. With right sides together, pin the wool front to the wool back along the side and bottom edges. Insert a label, pointing inward, in the seam. Stitch a ⅝in (1.5cm) seam, pivoting at the corners. Snip off the corners of the seam allowances. Press the seams open. Turn under and press ⅝in (1.5cm) on the top edge. Make the lining in the same way. With the wool right side out and the lining wrong side out, place the lining inside the wool, and pin the lining to the wool around the turned-under top edges.

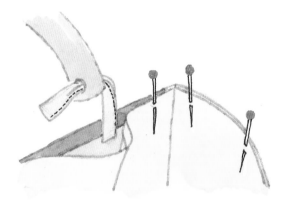

4 Make four loops from the lining fabric (see page 36, step 4) and thread them through the holes in the ends of the handles. To attach one handle to the front and the other to the back using loops, insert the loops between the bag and lining, with the ends overlapping the edge by ⅝in (1.5cm); the ends of each loop should be about ½in (1.2cm) apart. Pin and baste.

5 If your material is not too thick, you can topstitch all around the top edge. The fabric I used was too thick for this, so I slipstitched the lining in place and then hand-sewed both ends of each of the four handle loops in place securely using the tapestry yarn that matched the wool.

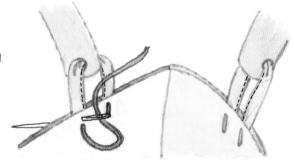

variation

The best thing about this bag is that there is no limit to the number of variations you can make when you are using French knots. Here a simple heart pattern has been used, with different-colored thread for each knot to give a fun multicolored look. Try sketching out a few ideas of your own and then stitch it onto the bag for a personalized touch.

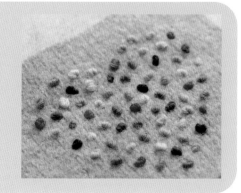

tweed & silk scarf purse

You can change the look of this soft purse by simply changing the scarf handle. The purse is made from a thick tweed fabric taken from an old coat (with the coat lining used to line the bag) and so is ideal for winter, but you could make a pretty summer version using linen or cotton and a floral scarf.

MATERIALS

2 pieces of tweed and 2 pieces of lining, each 16½ x 7in (42 x 17cm), for upper front and back

2 pieces of tweed and 2 pieces of lining, each 21 x 14in (54 x 35cm), for lower front and back

1 side-seam label (see page 121)

Matching sewing thread

Long silk scarf

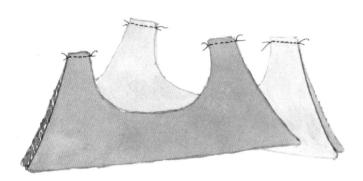

1 Using the templates on page 123, cut the upper front and back pieces and the lower front and back pieces to shape. With right sides together, pin the tweed upper front to the upper back at the two narrow top edges; stitch ⅜in (1cm) seams. Do the same for the lining upper front and back. Press the seams open.

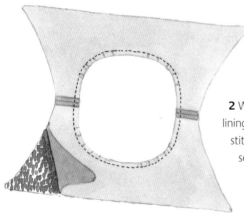

2 With right sides together, pin the lining to the tweed around the oval; stitch a ⅜in (1cm) seam. Clip into the seam allowance on the curves.

3 Turn the upper bag right side out, and press. Turn in ¼in (5mm) on both curved edges of the tweed and the lining; pin and topstitch close to the curved edges. Topstitch around the oval. Baste the tweed and lining together along the raw edges.

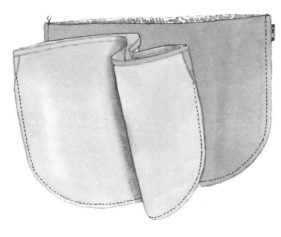

4 With right sides together, pin the tweed lower front and back together at the side and bottom edges. Insert a label, pointing inward, in the seam. Stitch a ⅜in (1cm) seam all around the curve. Pin and stitch the lining lower front and back together in the same way. Turn under and press a ⅜in (1cm) hem on the raw edge of the lining, and set the lining aside.

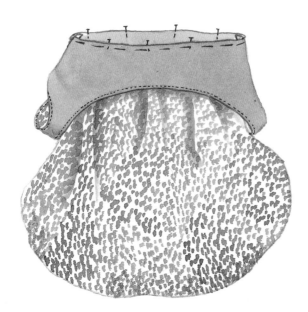

5 With the lower bag right side out and the upper bag with the lining on the outside, slip the upper bag over the lower bag so they are right sides together. With the raw edges even, pin them together all the way around, making small, evenly distributed pleats in the lower bag so it will fit. At the side seams, take care to overlap the points of the upper bag slightly. Stitch a ⅜in (1cm) seam. Press.

6 With the lining for the lower bag wrong side out, put it inside the tweed lower bag. Pin the turned-under top edge of this lining over the seam, pleating the lining fabric so it will fit. Slipstitch in place. Thread the scarf through the upper bag, tying the ends in a bow at one side.

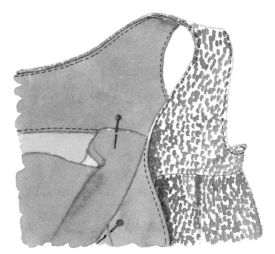

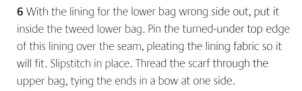

variation

This bag can be customized in an instant to go with any outfit due to the clever handle. Simply pick a scarf that matches your outfit and tie it around the loops at the top of the bag and it's ready to go! You don't have to just use scarves either—a long leather belt or some pretty cord would look great as well.

tweed & silk scarf purse **29**

plaid purse

An old blanket can provide a wonderful source of fabric for a winter purse. There will still be a lot of material left over after you make this purse, so hem the rest of the fabric and you will have a matching picnic blanket.

MATERIALS

1 piece of plaid wool and 1 piece of lining, each 18 x 21in (45.5 x 53.5cm), for front/back

1 side-seam label (see page 121)

1 short piece of narrow ribbon

Covered button (see page 119)

2 pieces of plaid wool, each 2 x 6in (5 x 15cm), for handle loops

1 piece of plaid wool, 2¾ x 24½in (7 x 62cm), for handle

4 pieces of plaid wool, each 14½ x 3in (37 x 8cm), for band and band lining

1 piece of plaid wool, 22 x 4¾in (56 x 12cm), for bow

1 piece of plaid wool, 4¼ x 4¾in (11 x 12cm), for bow center

Matching sewing thread

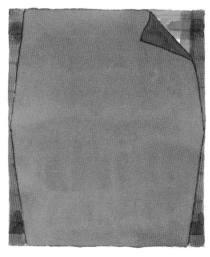

1 The front/back is cut as one piece. Fold the lining front/back piece in half crosswise and taper the sides so that it is 14½in (37cm) wide at the raw edges and 18in (45.5cm) wide at the fold, with a depth (from raw edges to fold) of 10½in (26.5cm). Open out the fabric and use it as a pattern to cut the wool front/back piece to shape. (The wool will be easier to cut unfolded, as a single thickness.)

2 Fold the wool front/back in half, with right sides together, and pin along the side edges. Insert a label, pointing inward, into the seam. Stitch ⅜in (1cm) seams. Snip off the corners of the seam allowances at the bottom corners. Repeat for the lining front/back. With the wool front/back right side out and the lining front/back wrong side out, put the lining inside the wool. Pin and baste the lining to the wool around the top edge.

3 Measure how long the ribbon will need to be to fit around the covered button, allowing for a ⅝in (1.5cm) seam allowance at each end; cut it to this length. Make the handle loops by folding the long edges in to meet at the center, wrong sides together, and then folding that in half lengthwise; slipstitch. Make the handle by turning under and pressing ¼in (5mm) along all four edges and then folding it in half lengthwise, wrong sides together; press and topstitch close to the edge down the length and across both ends.

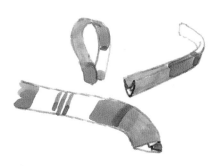

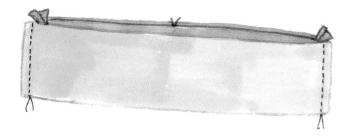

4 With right sides together, pin one band piece to another along the short edges. Stitch ⅜in (1cm) seams. Join the other two band pieces in the same way. Press. One of these pairs will be the outer band and the other will be the band lining. Put one inside the other, right sides together. Insert a handle loop, pointing downward, between the layers on the top edge at each side seam. Pin the ribbon loop, pointing downward, between the two layers at center back on the top edge.

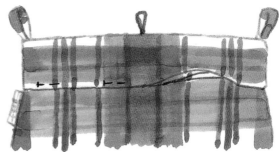

5 Pin the band lining to the outer band around the top edge, and stitch a ⅜in (1cm) seam. Press the seam. Open the band out flat. With the bag right side out, put the band inside the bag so that the right side of the band is against the wrong side of the bag. Pin and then stitch a ⅜in (1cm) seam.

6 Pull the band up out the bag, and press the seam toward the band. Turn under and press ⅜in (1cm) along the raw edge of the unfolded band. Fold the band in half, wrong sides together, along the seam joining the outer band and band lining. Pin the turned-under edge over the seam you have just stitched in step 5. Topstitch close to the edge. Remove the basting.

7 For the bow, fold the ends of the larger bow piece in to meet at the middle, right sides together. Stitch ¼in (5mm) seams along the top and bottom edges. Turn the bow right side out through the opening at the center, between the ends.

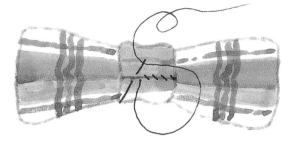

8 For the bow center, turn under the long edges to meet at the center, wrong sides together. With these raw edges on the underside, wrap this around the center of the bow and pin it at the back. Turn under the raw edges on the ends, and hand sew the ends together.

9 Hand sew the bow to the front of the bag, and hand sew the covered button at center front just above the bow. Thread the handle through the loops, and fold back each end. Pin and stitch across each end.

shoulder bags

leaf motif shoulder bag

Thick woolen fabrics make this a perfect shoulder bag for winter. For the main fabric I plundered the tweed from a skirt, and I used felted wool from an old rug for the leaves. If you don't have an old rug to cut up, you could felt an old sweater (see page 116). A button covered in the same fabric adds the finishing touch.

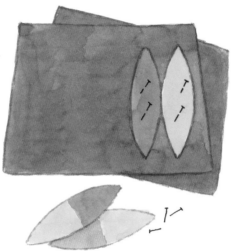

MATERIALS

2 pieces of main fabric and 2 pieces of lining fabric, each 15½ x 11¼in (39 x 29cm), for front and back

2 pieces of main fabric and 2 pieces of lining fabric, each 3½ x 19½in (9 x 50cm), for sides/base

4 pieces of felted wool, each 2½ x 8½in (6 x 21.5cm) in different colors, for leaves

1 side-seam label (see page 121)

1 shank button, ¾in (2cm) in diameter

Scrap of felted wool

1 piece of main fabric, 1⅜ x 4in (3.5 x 10cm), for button loop

2 pieces of main fabric, each 19 x 4½in (48 x 11cm), for handles

Matching sewing thread

1 Taper the sides of the four front and back pieces, so each is 14in (35.5cm) wide at the top and 16½in (42cm) wide at the bottom, with a depth of 11½in (29.5cm). Round off the bottom corners slightly. Using the leaf template on page 123, cut out four leaves from the felt. Pin the leaf shapes on the right side of the main fabric front, as shown. Topstitch close to the edge of each.

2 Place the two main-fabric side/base pieces with right sides together. At the wider end, pin and stitch a ⅝in (1.5cm) seam; press open. Now pin this around the side and bottom edges of the front, right sides together, aligning the ends with the top edge of the front. Insert a label, pointing inward, into the seam about 1½in (4cm) from the top; pin. Stitch a ⅝in (1.5cm) seam all around the side and bottom edges, curving the seam sharply at the corners. Clip into the seam allowance on the curves. Repeat to attach the other long edge of the side/base piece to the back. Press the seams flat.

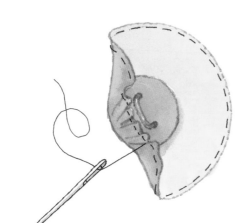

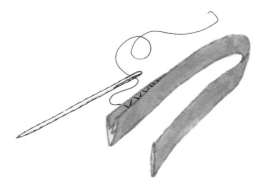

3 From the scrap of felted wool, cut a circle ⅝in (1.5cm) wider across than the button. Hand sew small running stitches close to the edge, put the button upside-down on the wrong side of the circle, and pull up the threads to gather the fabric smoothly around the button. Hand sew at the base to secure.

4 Fold the button-loop piece lengthwise so the raw edges meet at the center, and then fold it in half lengthwise. Slipstitch the folded edges together. Check that the loop is long enough to fit around the button, with a ⅝in (1.5cm) seam allowance at each end. Pin the loop at the center of the top edge of the bag back, on the right side, with the ends even with the raw edge of the back.

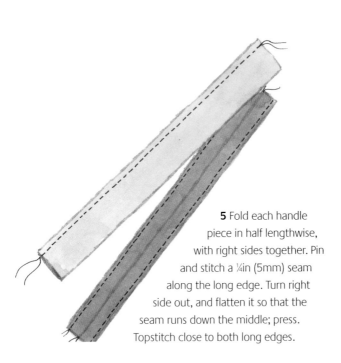

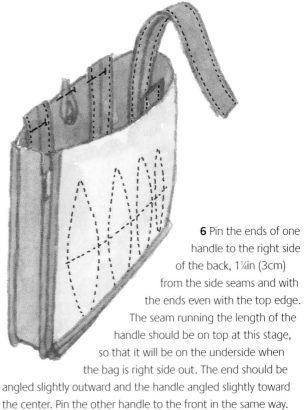

5 Fold each handle piece in half lengthwise, with right sides together. Pin and stitch a ¼in (5mm) seam along the long edge. Turn right side out, and flatten it so that the seam runs down the middle; press. Topstitch close to both long edges.

6 Pin the ends of one handle to the right side of the back, 1¼in (3cm) from the side seams and with the ends even with the top edge. The seam running the length of the handle should be on top at this stage, so that it will be on the underside when the bag is right side out. The end should be angled slightly outward and the handle angled slightly toward the center. Pin the other handle to the front in the same way.

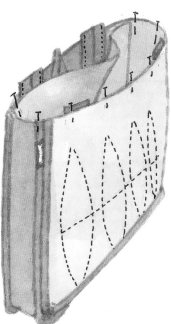

7 Assemble the lining as for the main fabric, step 2 (without the label) but leave a 4in (10cm) opening in one seam at the bottom. Turn the lining right side out. The main fabric should still be wrong side out. Insert the lining inside the main fabric, right sides together. With the raw edges even, pin them together around the top edge, and stitch a ⅝in (1.5cm) seam.

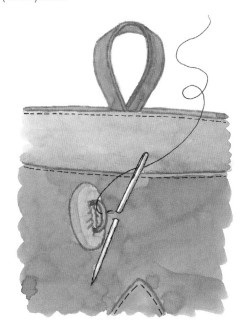

8 Turn the bag right side out through the opening in the bottom edge of the lining. Turn in the edges of the opening and slipstitch it closed. Press the seams, and push the lining inside the bag. Pin and topstitch close to the edge around the top. Sew the button to the outside of the front, to line up with the button loop.

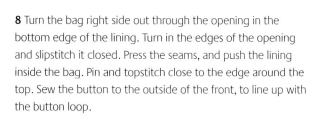

leaf motif shoulder bag **37**

velvet-topped print bag

I often use old skirts to make bags, and summery prints work especially well. However, there is not always enough material in a skirt to make a big bag, so for this design I have combined the fabric with some velvet from a scarf. A man's shirt in a vibrant color works well for the lining and a label. The velvet handles of the bag are attached by tabs and can be left long to make it a shoulder bag or shortened so it can be carried by hand.

MATERIALS

1 piece of print fabric 20 x 21in (51 x 53cm), for lower front/back

2 pieces of velvet, each 16½ x 6in (42 x 15cm), for upper front and upper back

2 pieces of lining fabric, each 20 x 17in (51 x 43cm)

1 side-seam label (see page 121)

4 pieces of velvet, each 3 x 4in (8 x 10cm), for tabs

2 pieces of velvet, each 2¾ x 32¼in (7 x 82cm), for handles

Matching sewing thread

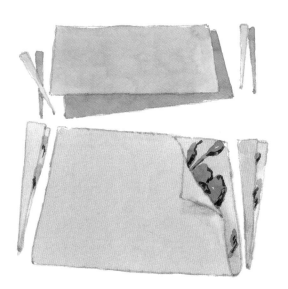

1 The lower front/back is cut as one piece. Fold the print fabric in half crosswise and taper the sides of the doubled-over print fabric so it is 16½in (42cm) wide at the top and 20in (51cm) wide at the fold, with a depth of 10½in (26.5cm) from raw edges to fold. Taper the sides of each velvet piece so it is 15in (38cm) wide at the top and 16½in (42cm) wide at the bottom, with a depth of 6in (15cm). Taper the sides of each lining piece so it is 15in (38cm) at the top and 20in (51cm) at the bottom, with a depth of 17in (43cm).

2 With right sides together, pin the lower edge of the velvet upper front to one top edge of the print piece; stitch a ⅝in (1.5cm) seam. Attach the velvet upper back to the other top edge of the print piece in the same way. Press the seams open. Now pin the front to the back at each side edge, with right sides together. Insert a label, pointing inward, in one of these seams, about 2in (5cm) from the top. Stitch ⅝in (1.5cm) seams. Press the seams open.

shoulder bags

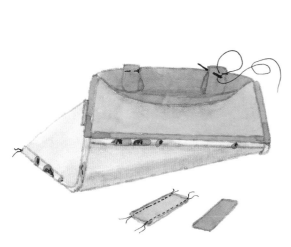

3 For the four tabs, fold each small piece of velvet in half lengthwise, right sides together. Pin and stitch a ¼in (5mm) seam down one long edge. Turn right side out, press, and fold in half crosswise. With raw edges even, pin two folded tabs to the top edge of the front and two to the top edge of the back on the right side, positioning them about 2¾in (7cm) from the edges. Baste the tabs in place.

4 Place the two lining pieces with right sides together, and pin along the side and bottom edges. Stitch a ⅝in (1.5cm) seam, pivoting at the corners and leaving a 4in (10cm) opening at the bottom. Press the seams and turn the lining right side out. With the main fabric still wrong side out, put the lining inside it so the right sides are together, and pin the lining to the velvet around the top edge. Stitch a ⅝in (1.5cm) seam. Turn the bag right side out through the opening in the lining. Turn in the edges of the opening, pin, and slipstitch it closed. Press the bag and push the lining inside it.

5 For the two handles, turn under and press ¼in (5mm) down the long edges, then fold each one in half lengthwise with wrong sides together; pin. Topstitch close to the edge, starting and stopping about 1½in (4cm) from the ends. Thread one handle through the loops on the front and the other through those on the back. With right sides together, pin the ends of the front handle together, and stitch a ⅝in (1.5cm) seam. Turn the raw edges to the inside, and topstitch the unstitched portion of the long edge. Repeat for the other handle. Slide the handles so the seams are hidden under a tab.

6 To use the bag as a shoulder bag leave the handles as they are, or arrange them as shown to carry the bag in your hand.

rose-trimmed burlap bag

MATERIALS

2 pieces of burlap (hessian), each 18 x 23in (46 x 58cm), for front and back

1 side-seam label (see page 121)

2 pieces of burlap, each 4 x 25in (10 x 63cm), for handles

6 pieces of cheesecloth (muslin) or marquisette (net), each 4 x 30in (10 x 77cm), for roses (if possible, cut so that one long edge of each is on selvage)

1 piece of cheesecloth or marquisette, 14 x 4in (36 x 10cm), for leaves

Matching sewing thread

I have made this elegant bag out of a thin burlap, though you could, of course, make it out of a different fabric. The delicate fabric of the roses contrasts beautifully with its rough texture.

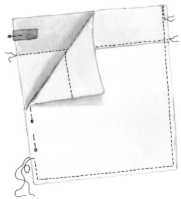

1 For the bag front and back, cut the two large pieces of burlap so that each is 46cm wide at the top, tapering to 42cm wide at the bottom, with a depth of 23in (58cm). Turn under and press ¼in (5mm) and then a further 4in (10cm) along the top edge of one of these pieces; pin. Trim the side edges of the hem even with the tapering sides of the bag, and then stitch the hem. Repeat for the other piece. With right sides together, pin the two pieces together. Insert a label in one side edge, pointing inward, and pin. Stitch a ⅝in (1.5cm) seam down both side edges and across the bottom, pivoting at the corners. Snip off the corners of the seam allowances. Zigzag stitch the raw edges of the seam together. Turn right side out and press.

2 For the handles, turn in ¼in (5mm) along all four edges of one burlap handle piece; press. Fold it in half lengthwise, wrong sides together; press. Pin and topstitch ⅛in (3mm) from the long edge. Repeat for the other handle. Pin one handle to the bag front, with the ends 4in (10cm) from the side edges, and even with the stitching of the hem on the front. Topstitch each end as shown. Attach the other handle to the back in the same way.

3 For each rose, wrap one strip around and around on itself, holding the raw edge at the base, and with the selvage at the top. Hand sew back and forth across the base, to cover the raw edges and prevent the rose from unwrapping. Repeat for the other five roses. From the remaining fabric, cut nine leaves, each about 1½ x 4in (4 x 10cm). Hand sew the base of one or two leaves with each rose to the hemmed portion of the bag front. Also use a few hand stitches to attach the other end of each leaf.

folk art wool bag

This embroidered motif was inspired by Scandinavian folk art. I cut up an old felted wool skirt to make the bag, but any thick woolen fabric would work, or you could felt the wool yourself (see page 116). The wool needs to be interfaced, and I used a woven nylon material salvaged from some old packaging, but you could use conventional interfacing or add extra body with fabric taken from, say, an old pillowcase.

MATERIALS

2 pieces of wool, 2 pieces of lining fabric, and 2 pieces of interfacing, each 13 x 12¾in (35.5 x 33cm), for front and back

Paper

Embroidery floss in selection of colors, such as light and dark orange, light and dark sage green, dark sage green, beige and white

1 piece of wool, 1 piece of lining fabric, and 1 piece of interfacing, each 13 x 4in (35.5 x 10cm), for base

2 pieces of wool, 2 pieces of lining fabric, and 2 pieces of interfacing, each 4 x 12¾in (10 x 33cm), for side panels

1 side-seam label (see page 121)

4 pieces of wool, each 2 x 2½in (5 x 6.5cm), for handle tabs

Old pair of hoop earrings or 2 D-rings

2 pieces of wool and 1 piece of interfacing, each 1½ x 24in (4 x 61cm), for handle

Small scrap of wool, to cover button

1¼in (3cm) covered-button kit

Matching sewing thread

Fabric marker (the vanishing type, which fades away after a few days) or tailor's chalk (which can be brushed away)

1 Taper the sides of the front and back pieces, so they are each 10⅜in (26.5cm) wide at the top and 14in (35.5cm) wide at the bottom, with a depth of 12¾in (33cm). Taper the side panels so they are each 3in (7.5cm) wide at the top and 4in (10cm) wide at the bottom, with a depth of 12¾in (33cm). Using the templates on page 123, cut out the bird, wing, and flower petal shapes from paper. With a ruler and fabric marker or tailor's chalk, on the right side of the wool front draw a vertical line down the center for the stem, starting 4in (10.5cm) from the top edge and finishing 2in (5.5cm) from the bottom edge. Repeat on the wool back.

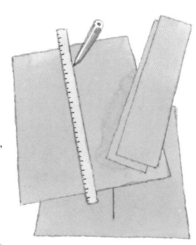

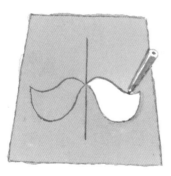

2 On both the front and the back, place the bird pattern on one side of the stem, 3½in (9cm) from the bottom edge, and draw around it using the marker. Turn it over and draw a mirror image of it on the other side of the stem. Use the wing pattern to draw a wing on each bird. Center the flower petal pattern above the vertical line, 1¾in (4.5cm) from the top, and draw around it. Draw two more petals flanking it. Farther down the stem, draw the curving lines for two pairs of leaves, and also give each bird two legs, plus tail feathers made from a clump of three lines.

3 Embroider the outlines of each bird with running stitch (see page 120), then fill in the body, but not the head, with equally spaced lines of running stitch following the outline, in a selection of colors. Add a French knot (see page 121) for an eye. Embroider the tail feathers with three straight stitches, the legs with running stitch, and the pairs of leaves with running stitch plus a French knot at the end. The flower petals are embroidered in the same way as the birds' bodies.

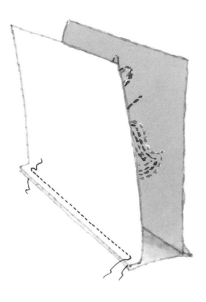

4 Interface the front, back, base, and side panels (see page 116). With right sides together, pin one long edge of the base to the bottom edge of the front. Stitch a ⅝in (1.5cm) seam, starting and stopping ⅝in (1.5cm) from the ends. Attach the other long edge of the base to the back in the same way. Press the seams away from the base.

5 Right sides together, pin the bottom edge of one side panel to one short edge of the base. Stitch a ⅝in (1.5cm) seam, starting and stopping ⅝in (1.5cm) from the ends, and pushing the existing seam allowances to one side. Attach the other side panel to the other short edge of the base in the same way. Pin one side panel to the front along the long edge of the panel, right sides together, pushing the seam allowances out of the way. Insert a label, pointing inward; pin. Stitch a ⅝in (1.5cm) seam, finishing ⅝in (1.5cm) from the bottom. Join the other long edge of this side panel to the back in the same way. Repeat to attach the second side panel to the front and back. Snip off seam allowance corners, and trim away interfacing seam allowances.

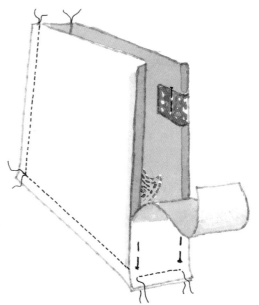

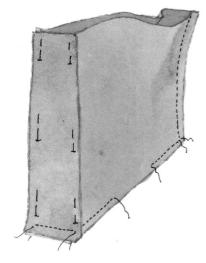

6 Repeat steps 4 and 5 (excluding interfacing and label) to make up the lining, leaving a 6in (15cm) opening in one of the base seams.

7 Cut the four handle-tab pieces to match the shape shown. They should be 2in (5cm) wide at the top and bottom, and 1½in (4cm) wide in the middle, with a depth of 2¾in (7cm). Place two pieces with right sides together, then pin and stitch a ¼in (5mm) seam along each long edge. Turn right side out and press. Fold the tab in half crosswise over a hoop earring or D-ring. Make the second tab in the same way.

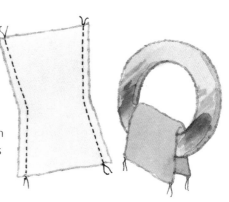

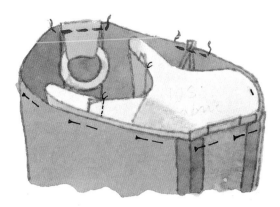

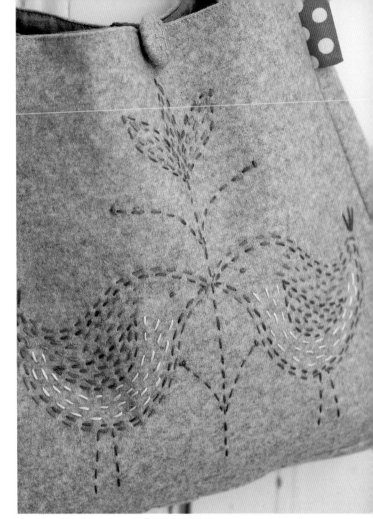

8 Pin each tab, pointing downward, to the top edge of one side panel on the right side, with the raw edges even; baste. Cut a 4¾in (12cm) length of embroidery floss and fold in half. Pin the loop, pointing downward, to the right side of the bag at center back of the top edge, with the ends even with the bag raw edge. Check that it will fit over the button when sewn on (see step 10), and then baste in place. With the wool wrong side out and the lining right side out, put the lining inside the wool. Pin them together around the top, and stitch a ⅝in (1.5cm) seam. Turn right side out through the opening in the lining. Turn in the edges of the opening, pin, and slipstitch it closed. Press the bag and then topstitch close to the top edge.

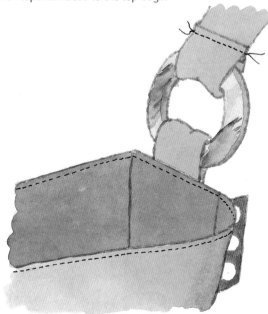

9 Interface one handle piece. Pin it to the other handle piece, right sides together, and stitch a ¼in (5mm) seam close to both long edges and one end. Snip off the corners of the seam allowances. Turn right side out and press. Turn in the raw edges of the open end, and pin. Insert one end of the handle through one of the rings on the bag, from the outside. Pin the end to the handle, and stitch in place. Repeat to attach the other end of the handle to the other ring.

10 Cut the scrap of wool to exactly the right size of circle for the covered-button kit, following the manufacturer's instructions. Embroider a motif on the center, making sure that the motif is smaller than the button. For the motif used here, work eyelet stitches —straight stitches that radiate out from the center—bringing the needle up through the middle each time, and then French knots at the ends. Cover the button (see page 119) and sew to the front at the center of the top edge.

monostrap sling bag

The flowing lines of the machine embroidery add to the graphic look of this stylish bag. It's inspired by backpacks but has just a single central strap, to wear over one shoulder. The strap at the front, which is designed to look like a continuation of the back strap, fastens through part of a recycled wooden-beaded necklace, but you could use an old buckle or wooden curtain ring instead. Or make a fabric loop to use with a covered button (see page 36, step 4, and page 120).

MATERIALS

2 pieces of thick wool or fleece and 2 pieces of lining fabric, each 11 x 18in (28 x 46cm), for front and back

1 piece of thick wool or fleece 4 x 24in (10 x 60cm), for back strap

1 piece of thick wool or fleece and 1 piece of lining fabric, each 2 x 4¼in (5 x 11cm), for front strap (see step 2)

1 side-seam label (see page 121)

Matching sewing thread

1 wooden buckle or curtain ring

Fabric marker that will fade or can be brushed away

1 On the bottom 6in (15cm) of the right side of the front, draw wavy lines using the fabric marker. Using a wide, close zigzag or satin stitch on your machine, stitch over the lines to create the machine-embroidered design.

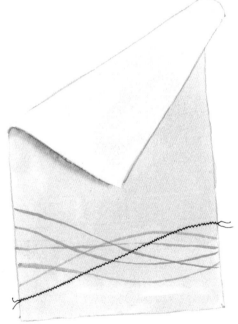

2 Fold the back strap in half lengthwise, wrong sides together. Pin and stitch a ¼in (5mm) seam down one side. Turn right side out. Refold the strap so that the seam runs down the middle; press. Turn in and press ¼in (5mm) at one end. The finished width of the front strap shown here is 1½in (4cm), but you may have to adjust the width to fit your buckle or curtain ring. With right sides together, pin the front strap lining piece to the wool piece along both long edges and one short edge. Stitch a ¼in (5mm) seam along these three edges. Turn right side out, and press.

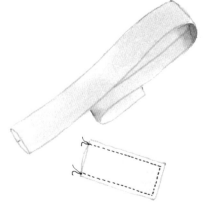

3 With right sides together, pin the wool front to the wool back along the side edges and bottom edge. Insert the back strap into the bottom seam at the center, pointing upward. If you have the bag back on top (wrong side up), then the seam on the strap should be on top; that way, the seam will be hidden when the bag is right side out. Also insert a label, pointing inward, in the side seam, near the bottom. Stitch a ⅝in (1.5cm) seam, pivoting at the corners. Snip off the corners of the seam allowances. Press the seams open.

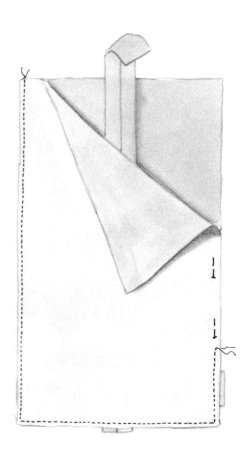

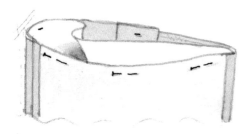

4 With right sides together, pin the lining front to the lining back along the side edges and bottom edge; stitch a ⅝in (1.5cm) seam, leaving a 4in (10cm) opening in the seam at the bottom edge. Press the seams and turn the lining right side out. Put it inside the wool bag, right sides together. Pin them together around the top edge. Insert the front strap into the seam, pointing downward, at center back, with the lining side of the strap against the bag lining, and the wool side of the strap against the wool bag. Stitch a ⅝in (1.5cm) seam.

5 Turn the bag right side out through the opening in the lining. Turn in the raw edges of the opening, pin, and slipstitch. About 12in (30cm) from the bottom, fold over the top to form a flap. At the back, turn under 1in (2.5cm) at the free end of the back strap; pin to the center of the back just below the fold; topstitch. At the front, sew on the buckle 5in (13cm) from the bottom edge.

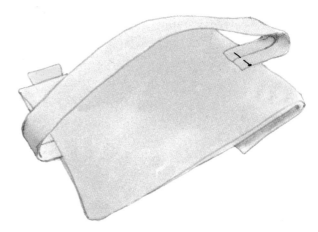

shoppers & totes

floral scrap tote

Over the years I have saved pretty floral fabrics from dresses, skirts, pillow covers, and tablecloths. Sometimes the piece is too small to make into an entire bag, so a great way to use up all these scraps is to make a bag from strips of contrasting fabrics cut to different widths. Using a selection of patterns can work really well together, but try to theme the colors. Lay out all your chosen fabrics and play around with the color combinations—you will know when you have got it right.

MATERIALS

Strips of fabric, each 2–4¼in (5–11cm) wide and 19in (48cm) long

2 pieces of cotton fabric, each 19 x 19in (48 x 48cm), for lining

2 pieces of main fabric and 2 pieces of cotton fabric, each 2¾ x 22½in (6.5 x 57cm), for handles

1 flat label (see page 121)

Matching sewing thread

1 For the front, pin the top strip to the second strip along the long edges with right sides together; stitch a ¼in (5mm) seam. Continue joining strips in this way until the front measures 19 x 19in (48 x 48cm). Make up the back in the same way. Cut out a 3¼in (8.5cm) square from each bottom corner of the front and back and also of the two lining pieces; the fabric between them will form the base.

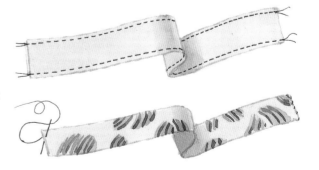

2 For each handle, pin a strip of main fabric to a strip of lining fabric with right sides together. Stitch a ¼in (5mm) seam along each long edge. Turn right side out and press. Turn in ¼in (5mm) at each end, press, and slipstitch.

3 With right sides together, pin the front to the back at the side and bottom edges; stitch ⅝in (1.5cm) seams. Repeat for the lining, but leave a 4in (10cm) opening in the bottom edge.

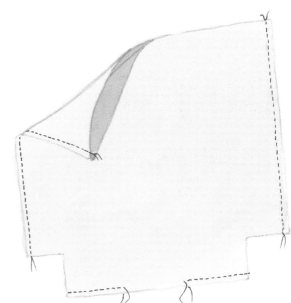

4 Flatten the base of the patchwork fabric so the seam runs along the middle. With right sides together, pin the base to the rest of the patchwork so the raw edges are even and the seam in the base aligns with the side seams. Stitch a ⅝in (1.5cm) seam on both edges. Press the seams open. Repeat for the lining. With the patchwork wrong side out and the lining right side out, place the lining inside the patchwork. Matching the side seams, pin them together around the top edge. Stitch a ⅝in (1.5cm) seam all around. Turn right side out through the opening in the lining. Turn in the edges of the opening, pin, and slipstitch closed.

5 Pin the ends of one handle to the right side of the front, 3in (7.5cm) from the side edges. Stitch as shown, close to the edges of the handle and through the handle, bag, and lining. Attach the other handle to the back of the bag in the same way. Pin the label in the center of the bag front, near the top, and topstitch.

tea-towel tote

Cotton or linen tea towels provide ideal fabric for shopping bags. Not only is the material sturdy but it often has very strong imagery, in a design that is just the right size and shape for a bag. I've used two tea towels for this bag: one for the front and back, and a second one that I've cut up for the decorative panels at the top and the tabs holding the wooden handles. To emphasize the theme of this bag, the handles are taken from wooden spatulas.

MATERIALS

2 tea towels

1 flat label (see page 121)

Matching and contrasting sewing thread

2 wooden spatula handles, each about 11in (28cm) long

1 From the first towel, cut two pieces, each 14¼ x 3¾in (36 x 9.5cm), for the panels, and four pieces, each 3½ x 8in (8.5 x 20cm), for the handle tabs, positioning them to make the most of the design. On one tab, turn under and press a single ¼in (5mm) hem on one long edge and a double ¼in (5mm) hem on the other long edge. Topstitch close to the double-hemmed edge only. Fold the tab in half crosswise, wrong sides together, and topstitch through the folded tab along the single-hemmed edge only. Repeat to make a second tab. Now make two more tabs in the same way but with the single and double hems on opposite edges to the first two tabs.

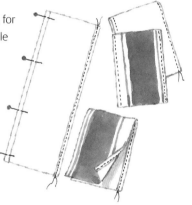

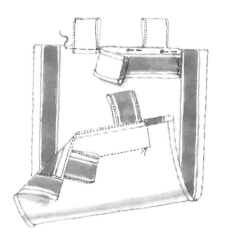

2 Pin and baste two tabs to the right side of one short edge of the second towel, with the ends overlapping the towel by ⅜in (1cm) and the open (double-hemmed) side edge toward the center. The tabs should be equidistant from the sides of the towel and about 6in (15cm) apart—far enough apart for the handles to fit inside (see step 3). Pin and baste the remaining two tabs to the other short edge in the same way. Turn under and press ½in (1cm) on the top edge of each panel and ¼in (5mm) on the other edges. Pin one panel to the right side of the second towel along one short edge, equidistant from the side edges and covering the ends of the tabs. Topstitch close to all four edges. Attach the second panel to the other short edge in the same way.

3 The motif of the flat label shown here uses a tight zigzag stitch in a contrasting thread. Fold the second towel in half, wrong sides together, and mark the position of the label at bottom right on the front. Unfold the towel, then topstitch the label in place. Fold the towel in half again, wrong sides together. Pin the side edges together and topstitch a ⅜in (1cm) seam along each, backstitching at the top to reinforce the seam. Insert one wooden handle through the front tabs and one through the back. Hand sew through the tabs directly under the handles.

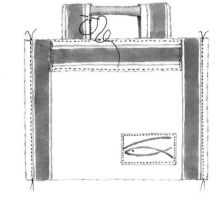

burlap & print shopper

This bag will take you to the grocery store, where you can fill it with carrots, potatoes, and onions, and then on to the chic cafe around the corner. Simply covering the utility burlap with material from a print chiffon blouse transforms the everyday into a stylish fashion statement.

MATERIALS

2 pieces of burlap (hessian), each 27¼ x 24in (69 x 60cm), for front and back underlayer

2 pieces of thin print fabric, each 27¼ x 16 (69 x 40cm), for front and back top layer

1 flat label (see page 121)

2 pieces of burlap and 2 pieces of thin print fabric, each 4¼ x 30in (11 x 76cm), for handles

Matching sewing thread

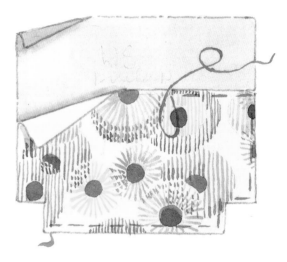

1 Cut 3½in (9cm) squares from the lower corners of the burlap front and back; the fabric between the cut-out squares will form the base of the bag. Repeat for the print front and back. With the lower raw edges even and wrong sides together, baste the print front to the burlap front around all four edges of the print piece. Repeat for the burlap and print backs.

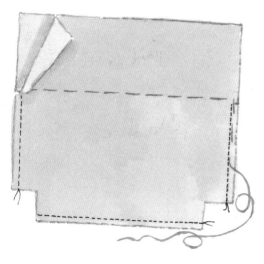

2 With right sides of the print together, pin the front to the back at the sides and lower edge. Stitch ⅝in (1.5cm) seams down the side edges and along the bottom, starting and stopping the stitching on the sides 8⅝in (21.5cm) from the top. Press the seams open, and clip into the seam allowances at the points where the stitching starts and ends.

shoppers & totes

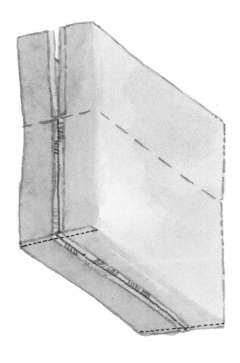

3 Flatten the base so the seam runs along the middle. With right sides together, pin the base to the rest of the bag so the raw edges are even and the seam in the base aligns with the side seams. Stitch a ⅝in (1.5cm) seam on both edges. Press the seams open, and zigzag stitch all the seam allowances.

4 Turn the bag right side out. With the unstitched side seam allowances turned to the outside, turn ⅝in (1.5cm) to the outside along the top edge of the burlap back; press. Turn a further 4in (10cm) to the outside, forming a burlap border that overlaps the raw edge of the print fabric by ⅝in (1.5cm); press. Repeat for the front. Pin both borders in place and topstitch close to the hemmed edge on both the front and back. Zigzag stitch the front and back borders together at the side edges using a wide, close stitch. Remove any visible basting.

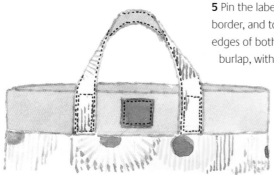

5 Pin the label to the right side of the bag front, in the center of the border, and topstitch. For each handle, turn under ⅜in (1cm) on all four edges of both the burlap and the print pieces. Pin the print to the burlap, with wrong sides together, and topstitch close to the long edges. Pin one handle to the front, with the ends even with the bottom of the border and 6¾in (17cm) from the sides. Topstitch as shown. Attach the other handle to the back in the same way.

MATERIALS

2 pieces of material, each 3½ x 45in (9 x 114cm), for handles

1 piece of paper, 16 x 27½in (41 x 70cm), for main panel

2 pieces of paper, each 4 x 11¾in (10 x 30cm), for side panels

Selection of paper scraps

Paper glue and masking tape

2 pieces of plastic sheeting, each 16⅝ x 28⅛in (42.5 x 71.5cm), for main panel

4 pieces of plastic sheeting, each 4⅝ x 12⅜in (11.5 x 31.5cm), for side panels

Matching sewing thread

packaging tote

This bag takes the word recycling literally, as it is made from the pieces of paper that usually end up in the recycling box, such as labels, stamps, postcards, printed paper bags, graphics from fruit crates, and old tickets. Before being sandwiched between clear plastic sheeting, the scraps have been stuck on plain white paper (one main piece forming the front, base, and back, and two more forming the side panels). However, you could use wrapping paper, wallpaper, or newspaper instead of paper. If you can't find a big-enough piece, stick two pieces together, and cover the seam with scraps. Similarly, if you can't find a long-enough piece of fabric for the handles (I cut up an old scarf), you can stitch two pieces together.

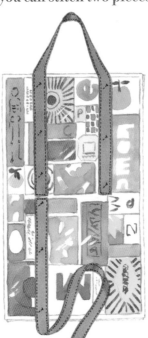

1 For each handle, turn under ¼in (5mm) on all four edges; press. Fold in half lengthwise, press, and baste. Mark the halfway point on your large piece of paper, and then arrange scraps on the top half, working downward from the top short edge till you get to the marked halfway point. Glue them in place. Turn the paper right around and stick scraps on the remaining area, again starting at the top, so that any directional scraps will be the right way up on the finished bag. Sandwich the paper between the two large pieces of plastic, with an equal amount of plastic extending beyond the paper all around. Pin the handles through all layers as shown, 3½in (9cm) from the side edges. Topstitch close to both long edges and both ends of one handle, stitching through the paper and plastic layers as well, and continuing the stitching through the looped part of the handle beyond the top of the bag. Repeat for the other handle. Remove basting.

2 Topstitch across both short edges of the bag ¼in (5mm) in from the edge of the plastic, stitching through the handles as well. Next, glue scraps to the two side panels of paper, working from top to bottom. Sandwich each between two pieces of plastic, with an equal amount of plastic all around; tape it in place. Topstitch across the top edge of each, ¼in (5mm) in from the edge of the plastic. Now pin each side panel to the front, wrong sides together, and with the top and side edges aligned. Remove tape, and stitch a seam down each side edge through the plastic, just outside the paper, stopping at the bottom edge of the paper. At the point where the stitching ends, clip into the plastic seam allowance of each side panel at right angles to the stitching.

3 To create the base, make two parallel folds across the width of the main panel, 2in (5cm) either side of the center mark. In other words, the first fold should be even with the bottom edge of the paper of each side panel, and the second fold 4in (10cm) away from the first. With wrong sides together, pin the bottom edge of one side panel to the edge between the folds; stitch a seam through the plastic, just outside the paper, starting at the

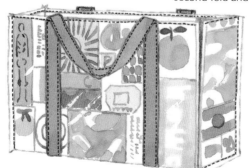

second fold and stitching as far as the first fold. At the starting point of the seam, clip into the plastic seam allowance of the side panel, at right angles to the stitching. Join the other side panel to the base in the same way. Now pin one side panel to the bag back along the side edges, wrong sides together. Stitch a seam through the plastic, just outside the paper, starting at the top edge and stitching as far as the fold. Repeat for the other side panel.

curtain fabric shopper

Old curtains made from sturdy, closely woven decorator fabric are an ideal source of fabric for shopping bags. If the fabric is heavy enough, you don't have to line the bag. Here I have used an old polka-dot T-shirt to line just the top and handles, providing a flash of contrast with the chintz.

MATERIALS

2 pieces of main fabric, each 21 x 17in (54 x 43cm)

1 flat label (see page 121)

2 pieces of lining fabric, each 21 x 7in (54 x 18cm)

2 pieces of main fabric and 2 pieces of lining fabric, each 3 x 25½in (7.5 x 65cm), for handles

Matching sewing thread

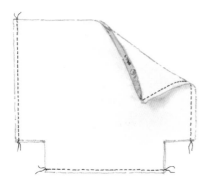

1 Cut a 3½in (9cm) square from the bottom corners of both main fabric pieces; the fabric between will form the base of the bag. Place the two pieces with right sides together. Pin and stitch ⅝in (1.5cm) seams along both side edges and along the bottom edge. Press the seams open.

2 Flatten the base so that the seam runs along the middle. With right sides together, pin the base to the rest of the bag so that the raw edges are even and the seam in the base aligns with the side seams. Stitch a ⅝in (1.5cm) seam on both edges. Press the seams open, and zigzag stitch all the seam allowances. Turn right side out. Pin the label at center front, on the right side near the top, and topstitch.

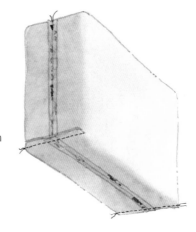

3 Place the two lining pieces with right sides together. Pin and stitch ⅝in (1.5cm) seams at both side edges; press the seams open. Turn under and press a double ¼in (5mm) hem along the lower edge of the lining; stitch. With the lining wrong side out, slip it over the main fabric, so the right sides are together. With the raw edge of the lining even with the top of the main fabric, and the side seams aligning, pin and stitch a ⅝in (1.5cm) seam around the top. Push the lining inside, and press the top edge.

4 For each handle, pin one of the main-fabric handle pieces to one of the handle lining pieces with right sides together. Stitch a ¼in (5mm) seam along each long edge. Turn right side out and press. Turn in the raw edges at the ends and press. Pin the ends of the handles to the right side of the front, equidistant from the side edges and with the ends 4in (10cm) from the top edge. Stitch as shown, close to the edge of the handle, stitching through the handle, bag, and lining. Attach the other handle to the back of the bag in the same way.

fold-up shopper

Keep this fold-up shopper in your purse and you'll always be prepared for those unplanned purchases. It's also great for stashing away in a suitcase, as it's lightweight and compact when folded up yet roomy and surprisingly sturdy when put to use. And it's so quick to make that you could give them as gifts.

MATERIALS

2 pieces of muslin, each 20 x 17in (50 x 43cm), for front and back

2 pieces of muslin, each 2¾ x 15in (7 x 39cm), for handles

1 piece of muslin, 1⅜ x 2¾in (3.5 x 7cm), for button loop

2 pieces cut from a tea towel, each 16¼ x 5in (41 x 13cm), for borders

1 button

Matching sewing thread

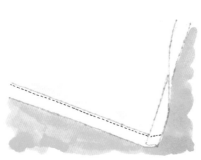

1 Place the front and back with wrong sides together and raw edges even. Turn under and press both layers to form a double ⅜in (1cm) hem on the right side of the back piece along the side and bottom edges. Pin and then stitch close to the edge of the hem. Turn ⅝in (1.5cm) to the right side along the top edge of the front and back; press.

2 Turn under and press ¼in (5mm) along the long edges of each handle. Fold the handle in half lengthwise, wrong sides together, and press. Pin and topstitch close to the hemmed edge. Pin the ends of one handle to the right side of the back at the top edge, 3½in (9cm) from the side edges, with the ends overlapping the turned-under top edge of the bag front by ⅝in (1.5cm)—in other words, the raw edges are even. Baste. Pin and baste the other handle to the back in the same way.

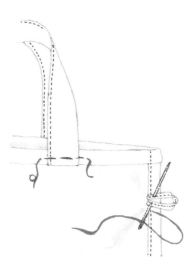

3 Make the button loop from the small piece of muslin by folding both long edges into the center and then folding it in half lengthwise. Press, pin, and topstitch close to the edge. Fold the loop in half and pin it, pointing outward, to the right side of the muslin at one side edge, 2⅛in (5.5cm) from the top edge, so the ends overlap the edge by ⅜in (1cm). Check that it will fit around the button, and then baste in place.

4 Turn under and press ⅜in (1cm) on all four edges of each border piece. Pin one border, right side up, to the right side of the front at the top edge, over the ends of the handle. Topstitch along both long edges of the border, stitching through the handle as well at the top edge. Attach the other border to the back in the same way.

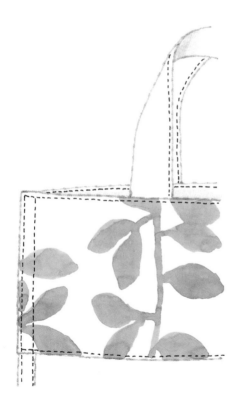

5 Pin and topstitch parallel to the short edges of the border, stitching through both the front and back at once, and lining up this stitching with the stitching on the hemmed muslin. Stitch again along the short edges of the border, but this time close to the edge. Continue the stitching down one side edge of the muslin, across the bottom and up the other side edge, so that you have a double row of stitching through the hemmed portion of the muslin and border. Press the bag, remove basting, and sew the button at center front, halfway between the top and bottom edges of the border.

6 To fold up the bag, tuck the handles inside and fold up the muslin portion so that only the border is visible and the button is on top. Fold it in half and then fold in the sides with the button and loop so they meet in the center and can be fastened.

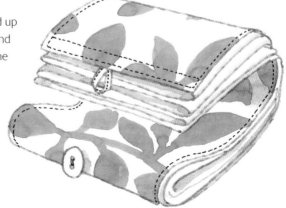

canvas beach bag

This capacious bag is immensely useful for days at the beach, when you have to take a pile of towels, swimwear, suntan lotion, a picnic, and a blanket with you! I made it from an old windbreak, so the fabric is very strong and has that lovely faded look of the seaside. A worn-out deckchair could also be plundered for its canvas, or sturdy curtain material or a heavy tablecloth could be used instead. Plastic-covered cardboard inside a canvas sleeve provides a sturdy, waterproof base for transporting soggy towels and sandy shoes.

MATERIALS

1 piece of canvas, 15 x 45½in (38 x 116cm), for front/base/back

2 pieces of canvas, each 15 x 16½in (38 x 42cm), for side panels

1 piece of canvas, 15 x 14½in (38 x 37cm), for base lining

2 pieces of canvas, each 5 x 21½in (13 x 55cm), for handles

1 side-seam label (see page 121)

Matching sewing thread

1 piece of stiff cardboard covered in a sturdy plastic bag

1 The long piece of canvas will form the front, base, and back. With right sides together and top edges even, pin one long edge of one side panel to one side edge of the long piece; stitch a ⅝in (1.5cm) seam, stopping the stitching ⅝in (1.5cm) from the bottom edge of the side panel. Clip into the seam allowances of both pieces at this point.

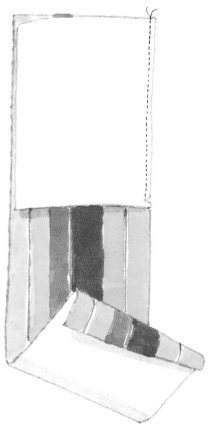

2 In the same way, pin the other long edge of this side panel to the same side edge of the long piece, with right sides together and top edges even. Check that the portion between these two side seams will fit exactly on the base (but don't stitch it yet), and then stitch the pinned seam and clip into the seam allowances as in step 1.

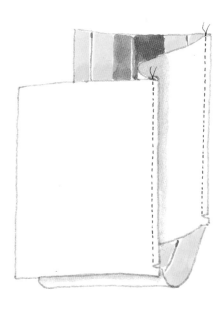

3 Repeat steps 1 and 2 to attach the other side panel to the other side edge of the long piece. Zigzag stitch all the seam allowances and press the seams open.

4 Turn under and press a double ⅜in (1cm) hem on the two long edges of the base lining; stitch. With wrong sides together and raw edges even, place the base lining over the base. Pin the short edge of the base lining to one side edge of the base and also to the bottom edge of one side panel, between the clips; baste. Stitch a ⅝in (1.5cm) seam between the clips through all three layers. It's easiest to start at the center and stitch into one corner, and then start at the center again and stitch into the other corner. Repeat to attach the other short edge of the base lining to the other side edge of the base and the bottom edge of the other side panel.

5 Turn under and press ¼in (5mm) and then 2½in (6.5cm) all around the top edge of one handle; baste. Topstitch in place. Turn under ¼in (5mm) on all four edges, and fold the handle in half lengthwise, wrong sides together. Topstitch close to the turned-under edges. Repeat for the other handle.

6 Pin each end of one handle to the outside of the front panel, 2in (5cm) from the side seams, with the bottom even with the top hem; topstitch as shown. Attach the second handle to the back in the same way, inserting a side-seam label between the outside edge of the handle and the bag prior to stitching. Insert the piece of cardboard or plastic between the base and the base lining through one of the unstitched sides of the base lining.

patchwork weekender

This generous-size bag is ideal for using up small scraps of material, and the patchwork is quick to do on the sewing machine. Choose patterns that are all quite different (such as stripes, checks, florals, and polkadots in a variety of scales) but are in your chosen color palette, so that they both contrast and harmonize. For the sides, base, and handles, I used some suedette taken from a pillow cover, but any sturdy solid-color fabric would work. For the bag to keep its shape, it needs to be interfaced (see page 116), but you could use recycled fabric for the interfacing and a recycled zipper, too, if you wish.

MATERIALS

1 piece of cardboard, 8¼ x 6¼in (21 x 16cm)

Scraps of contrasting fabrics for patches, for front and back

1 flat label (see page 121)

2 pieces of lining fabric and 2 pieces of interfacing, each 22¼ x 16¼in (57 x 42cm), for front and back

2 pieces of solid-color fabric, 2 pieces of lining fabric, and 2 pieces of interfacing, each 7½ x 10¾in (19 x 27.5cm), for sides

1 piece of solid-color fabric, 1 piece of lining fabric, and 1 piece of interfacing, each 22½ x 7½in (57 x 19cm), for base

2 pieces of solid-color fabric, each 2¼ x 27½in (6 x 70cm), for handles

Matching sewing thread

1 zipper about 19in (48cm) long

2 pieces of ¼in (6mm) tubing, each 21½in (55cm) long

1 Draw around the piece of cardboard and cut out 18 patches. Decide on the arrangement: you need three rows of three for the front and the same for the back. Pin two together along one short edge, right sides together, and stitch a ⅝in (1.5cm) seam. Join another one to the first two in the same way. Repeat to make five more strips of three patches each. Press all the seams open.

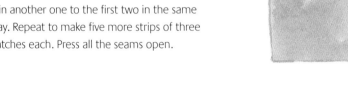

2 With right sides together, pin the bottom edge of the upper row to the top edge of the middle row, matching seams. Stitch a ⅝in (1.5cm) seam. In the same way, join the top edge of the lower row to the bottom edge of the middle row. Press the seams open. This will be the front. Now join three more strips in the same way to make the back.

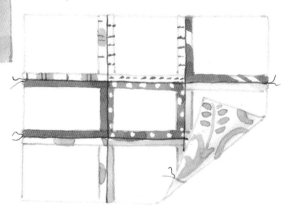

3 Pin the label to the right side at center front, about 2½in (6.5cm) from the top edge; topstitch around all four edges of the label. Mark a point on each side edge of the patchwork front and back, 9½in (24.5cm) from the bottom. Taper the sides above the marked points up to the top edge, so the width at the top is 20in

(51cm). Use this as a template to cut the lining and interfacing fronts and backs to shape. Using the triangular template on page 124, cut the solid-color, lining, and interfacing side pieces to shape. Interface the patchwork front and back, and the solid-color base and side triangles (see page 116).

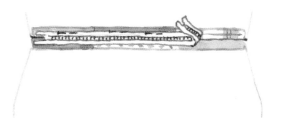

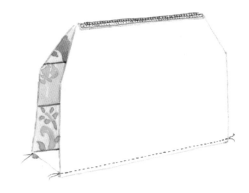

4 With right sides together, pin the front to the back along the top edge; machine baste a ⅝in (1.5cm) seam. Press the seam flat and open out the pieces. Center the closed zipper, face down, over the basted seam on the wrong side; pin and hand baste the zipper in place near the edges of the zipper tape. With the pieces right side up and the zipper foot on the machine, topstitch down both sides of the zipper about ¼in (5mm) from the seam. Remove all the basting.

5 Pin one long edge of the base to the lower edge of the front, with right sides together. Stitch a ⅝in (1.5cm) seam, starting and stopping the stitching ⅝in (1.5cm) from the ends. Join the other long edge of the base to the lower edge of the back in the same way. Press the seams open.

6 With right sides together, pin the bottom edge of one side triangle to one side edge of the base. Stitch a ⅝in (1.5cm) seam, starting and stopping the stitching ⅝in (1.5cm) from the ends. It's best to start in the middle and stitch into one corner, and then go back to the middle and stitch into the other corner.

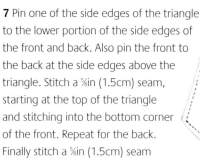

7 Pin one of the side edges of the triangle to the lower portion of the side edges of the front and back. Also pin the front to the back at the side edges above the triangle. Stitch a ⅝in (1.5cm) seam, starting at the top of the triangle and stitching into the bottom corner of the front. Repeat for the back. Finally stitch a ⅝in (1.5cm) seam above the triangle. Open the zipper, and attach the other triangle to the other side edge of the base, front, and back in the same way. Press the seams open and turn right side out.

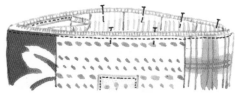

8 Repeat steps 5, 6, and 7 to make the lining, but do not turn right side out. Turn under and press ⅝in (1.5cm) around the top edge. Place the lining inside the patchwork, wrong sides together, and pin it in place around the top edge, below the zipper. Baste and then topstitch. Remove the basting.

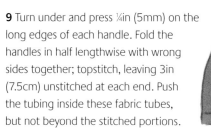

9 Turn under and press ¼in (5mm) on the long edges of each handle. Fold the handles in half lengthwise with wrong sides together; topstitch, leaving 3in (7.5cm) unstitched at each end. Push the tubing inside these fabric tubes, but not beyond the stitched portions. Flatten out the unstitched ends of each handle so that the seam on the portion with the tubing is at center back of the handle. Turn under and press a narrow hem on the raw edge at each flat end.

10 With the three pressed-under edges turned under, pin the flat ends of one handle to the right side of the front, and pin the flat ends of the other handle to the right side of the back. Topstitch around all three edges of each flat end.

oilcloth shopper

I made this out of an old oilcloth tablecloth—it makes a good, strong shopping bag that is also practical and wipe-clean. In fact, modern oilcloth is no longer oiled canvas but simply vinyl on a webbing backing. Vinyl-coated cotton is similar. Another alternative would be to use a regular cotton tablecloth and line it with polythene.

MATERIALS

1 piece of oilcloth, 44 x 13in (113 x 33cm), for front/base/back

2 pieces of oilcloth, each 13 x 16¾in (33 x 43cm), for side panels

1 piece of oilcloth, 13 x 13in (33 x 33cm), for base lining

2 pieces of oilcloth, each 4½ x 27in (11 x 68cm), for handles

1 side-seam label (see page 121)

Matching poly/cotton sewing thread

Tissue paper or masking tape (optional)

1 piece of stiff plastic or cardboard, 11¾ x 11¾in (30 x 30cm)

1 When working with oilcloth, use a size 16 needle and a long stitch length. You shouldn't have a problem with it sliding when stitching with it wrong side up. To help stop it from sliding when topstitching, either place tissue paper between the oilcloth and the presser foot, or stick masking tape to the underside of the presser foot. You can't press oilcloth, but laying it flat in a warm place should help remove any creases. The long piece of oilcloth will form the front, base, and back. With right sides together and top edges even, pin one long edge of one side panel to one side edge of the long piece; stitch a ⅝in (1.5cm) seam, stopping the stitching ⅝in (1.5cm) from the bottom edge of the side panel. Clip into the seam allowances of both pieces at this point.

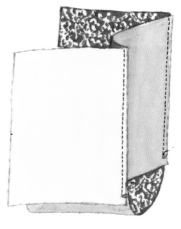

2 In the same way, pin the other long edge of this side panel to the same side edge of the long piece, with right sides together and top edges even. Check that the portion between these two side seams will fit exactly on the base (but don't stitch it yet). Stitch the pinned seam and clip into the seam allowances as in step 1.

3 Repeat steps 1 and 2 to attach the other side panel to the other side edge of the long piece. Now with wrong sides together and raw edges even, place the base lining over the base. Pin one edge of the base lining to one side edge of the base and also to the bottom edge of one side panel, between the clips; baste. Stitch a ⅝in (1.5cm) seam between the clips through all three layers. (It's easiest to start at the center and stitch into one corner, and then start at the center again and stitch into the other corner.) Repeat to attach the opposite edge of the base lining to the other side edge of the base and the bottom edge of the other side panel.

4 Turn under a 3in
(7.5cm) hem all
around the top
edge; baste. Topstitch in
place. Turn under ¼in (5mm) on
all four edges of one handle, and fold the handle in half
lengthwise, wrong sides together. Topstitch close to the
turned-under edges. Repeat for the other handle.

5 Pin the ends of one handle
to the outside of one side
panel, 2in (5cm) from the side
seams, with the bottoms even
with the top hem; topstitch
as shown. Attach the
second handle to the
other side panel in the
same way, inserting a side-
seam label between the
outside edge of the handle and the bag prior to stitching. Insert
the piece of cardboard or plastic between the base and the base
lining through one of the unstitched sides of the base lining.

oilcloth shopper **79**

soft floral bag

This soft, vintage-style bag was made from an old skirt. The skirt was lined, and the lining made an ideal fabric with which to line the bag. Although it is meant to be soft, you may still want to interface it (see page 116) to make it firmer. I covered the buttons in the same fabric as the bag, which adds nice detailing, and the label gives a designer touch.

MATERIALS

4 pieces of main fabric, each 12½ x 4in (32 x 10cm), for band

1 side-seam label (see page 121)

2 pieces of main fabric and 2 pieces of lining fabric, each 16 x 11¾in (41 x 30cm), for front and back

2 pieces of main fabric and 2 pieces of lining fabric, each 2½ x 23in (6.5 x 58.5cm), for handles

Scrap of main fabric, and 4 buttons with shanks or 4 covered button kits

Matching sewing thread

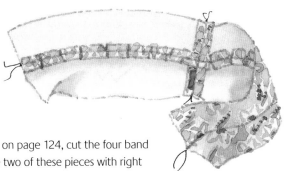

1 Using the template on page 124, cut the four band pieces to shape. Place two of these pieces with right sides together, and pin at one end. Insert a label in the seam, pointing inward. Stitch a ⅝in (1.5cm) seam, open out flat, and press the seam open. Assemble the two remaining band pieces in the same way, but without the label. With right sides together, raw edges even, and seams matching, pin together along the top edge (the shorter of the two long edges). Stitch a ⅝in (1.5cm) seam. Clip into the seam allowances on the curves. Open out flat and press the seam open.

2 Using the template on page 122, round off the lower corners on the front and back pieces. Using pins or a fabric marker, mark four fold lines for two pleats at the top edge of the main fabric 3in (7.5cm), 3½in (9cm), 5in (12.5cm), and 5½in (14cm) from one side edge; mark four more fold lines for the other two pleats the same distances from the other side edge. With right sides together and raw edges even, pin the front to the back around the sides and bottom. Stitch a ⅝in (1.5cm) seam, curving the stitching around the bottom corners. Press the seams, and clip into the seam allowances on the curves. Assemble the lining in the same way.

3 Turn the main fabric right side out and the lining wrong side out. Put the lining inside the main fabric, wrong sides together. With the raw edges even, pin and baste around the top edge. At the fold lines, make pleats in the lined top edge as shown, pin, and then baste.

4 With the band opened out, pin one long edge of the band to the top edge of the lined bag, right sides together and matching the side seams. Right sides together, pin the ends of the opened-out band together, adjusting the width of the seam so that the band will fit smoothly around the top of the bag. Remove enough pins from the pinned top seam to allow you to stitch the seam joining the ends of the band. After stitching it, press open the seam, and then re-pin the band to the top of the bag. Stitch a ⅝in (1.5cm) seam around the top. Press the seam.

5 Press under ⅝in (1.5cm) on the remaining raw edge of the band. Fold the top half of the band to the inside along the seamline. Pin the turned-under edge to the inside of the seam you've just stitched in step 4. Baste, and then topstitch in place from the right side of the band.

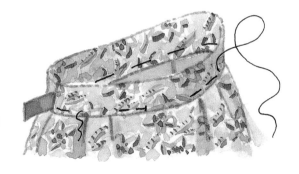

6 For the handles, pin each main piece to a lining piece with right sides together. Stitch a ¼in (5mm) seam down both long edges and one end. Turn right side out and turn in ¼in (5mm) at the remaining end; slipstitch the end. Gather up the ends of one handle so they are no wider than the buttons, and pin them to the outside of the front band, centering them between the top and bottom edges of the band and between the pleats; topstitch. Attach the other handle to the back band in the same way. Cover the four buttons (see page 119) and sew them on top of the ends of the handles. Remove basting and press the bag.

vintage silk scarf bag

Combine a vintage silk scarf and a pair of delicate wooden handles to create a glamorous and glossy silk bag in next to no time. Pretty floral scarves from the 1960s or vibrant abstract designs from the '70s look especially good. I like to emphasize the floaty look of the silk by leaving it unlined, though if you want your bag to be sturdier you could adapt the instructions for lining the Wooden-Handle Purse (see page 10).

MATERIALS

1 large square silk scarf

1 side-seam label (see page 121)

Matching sewing thread

Thin tracing paper or tissue paper (optional)

1 pair of wooden handles

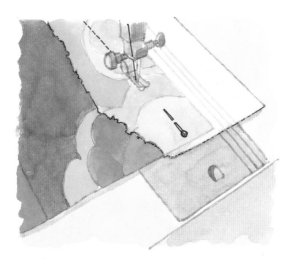

1 Fold the scarf in half, right sides together. Pin along each side edge, and insert a label on one side, pointing inward. Stitch a ⅝in (1.5cm) seam along each side edge, stopping 5½in (14cm) from the top. (To make it easier to stitch on very fine fabric, place thin tracing paper or tissue paper between the machine and the fabric, and then tear it away afterward.)

2 Wrap one top edge over one wooden handle, wrong sides together. Pin it in place at least 1in (2.5cm) below the handle, and then baste. Repeat for the remaining top edge and other handle. Stitch, flattening the material as you sew and then bunching up the sewn portion. Hand sew a few stitches at each end, to join the fabric tightly together under the handle, helping it stay in place. Repeat for the other top edge and handle. Turn the bag right side out, remove basting, and press using a cool iron.

pearl button evening bag

MATERIALS

4 pieces of silky fabric and 2 pieces of interfacing, each 9½ x 8¼in (24.5 x 21cm)

Pearl buttons

2 pieces of silky fabric, each 5½ x 16in (14 x 40cm), for handles

Scrap of fabric for covering button

Covered-button kit

Small piece of narrow ribbon to match

Matching sewing thread

This gorgeous, elegant evening bag uses lots of pearl buttons, so keep an eye out for them at thrift shops, flea markets, and garage sales. The buttons used here came from a pillow cover and a purse covered in pearl buttons that I came across, and I combined them with a silky fabric from a pair of pajamas. The number of buttons you'll need depends on their size, but the ones here are about half an inch (1.5cm) wide and I used nearly 250—sewing them on is a good project for when you are watching television!

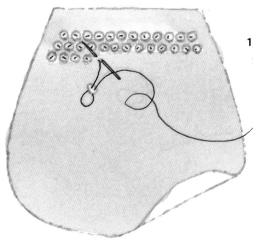

1 Using the template on page 125, cut the four pieces of fabric to shape. Interface two of the pieces (see page 116). Sew on buttons to cover the right side of one interfaced piece, leaving ¾in (2cm) free of buttons all around the edges.

2 With right sides together, pin the piece with the buttons to the other interfaced piece around the side and bottom edges. Stitch a ⅝in (1.5cm) seam all around, being careful to avoid the buttons. Trim away the interfacing seam allowances. Clip into the seam allowances on the curves. Press the seam open and press under ¼in (5mm) at the top edge. Repeat for the two remaining pieces, to make the lining.

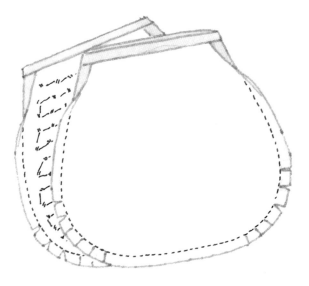

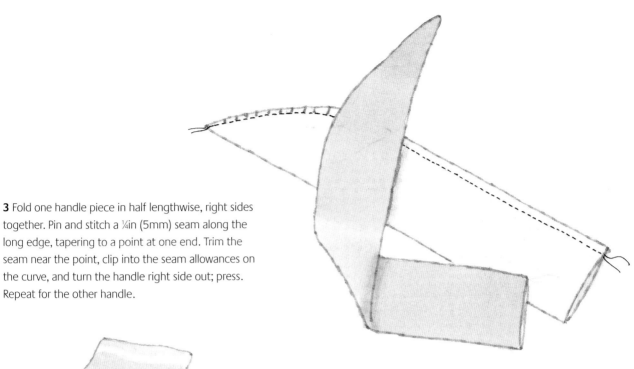

3 Fold one handle piece in half lengthwise, right sides together. Pin and stitch a ¼in (5mm) seam along the long edge, tapering to a point at one end. Trim the seam near the point, clip into the seam allowances on the curve, and turn the handle right side out; press. Repeat for the other handle.

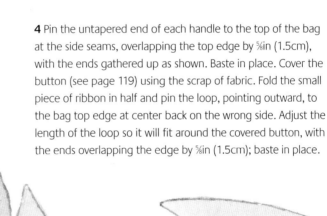

4 Pin the untapered end of each handle to the top of the bag at the side seams, overlapping the top edge by ⅝in (1.5cm), with the ends gathered up as shown. Baste in place. Cover the button (see page 119) using the scrap of fabric. Fold the small piece of ribbon in half and pin the loop, pointing outward, to the bag top edge at center back on the wrong side. Adjust the length of the loop so it will fit around the covered button, with the ends overlapping the edge by ⅝in (1.5cm); baste in place.

5 With the main fabric right side out and the lining wrong side out, put the lining inside the main fabric. Pin and baste the turned-under top edges together, and then topstitch close to the edge all around. Remove the basting, and press. Sew the covered button at the top at center front. Tie the handles together at one side.

evening bag with beaded handle

Here's a good way to use a top you bought for the fabric but then found that it didn't suit you. The blouse I used here had a pretty retro pattern, with an old string of beads forming the handle. The lining came from a shirt, and even the ribbon loop is recycled, as it was a hanging loop inside an old top. A glass button gives the bag a final touch of glamour.

MATERIALS

2 pieces of main fabric and 2 pieces of lining fabric, each 8¼ x 8¾in (21 x 22cm)

1 side-seam label (see page 121)

Scraps of main fabric

Matching sewing thread

String of beads

Piece of ribbon for loop

1 glass button

1 Taper the sides of the pieces so they are 7½in (19cm) wide at the top, and 9in (23cm) wide at the bottom, with a depth of 8½in (22cm). Place the two main pieces with right sides together, and pin down the sides and across the bottom. Insert a label, pointing inward, in one side seam; pin. Stitch a ⅝in (1.5cm) seam along the sides and bottom, pivoting the stitching at the corners. Snip off the corners of the seam allowances. Repeat for the two lining pieces, but leave a 4in (10cm) opening in the seam at the bottom.

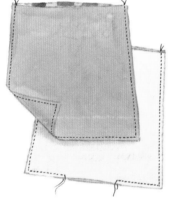

2 Cut the string of beads to the right length for a handle, leaving about 1½in (4cm) of extra thread. Cut two scraps of main fabric, each about ¾ x 1¼in (2 x 3cm). Fold each one in half lengthwise and tie the extra thread at the end of the beads to it, leaving about ⅛in (3mm) between the fabric and the first bead. Hand sew each piece of fabric to the right side of the main fabric at each side seam, keeping it entirely within the ⅝in (1.5cm) seam allowance. Fold the piece of ribbon in half and pin it to the right side of the back at the center of the top edge, with the loop pointing inward and the ends of the ribbon even with the raw edge.

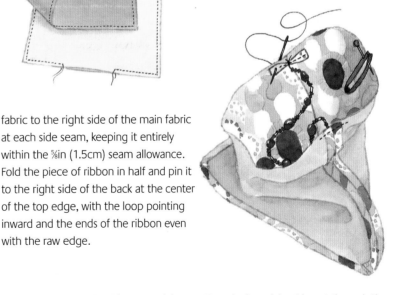

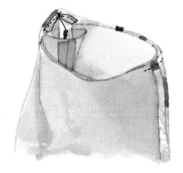

3 Turn the lining right side out and the main fabric wrong side out. Place the lining inside the main fabric, so that right sides are together. With the side seams matching, pin the two sections together around the top edge. Stitch a ⅝in (1.5cm) seam, being careful to keep the beads entirely below the seamline.

Turn the bag right side out through the opening in the bottom edge of the lining, and press. Turn in the edges of the opening, pin, and slipstitch it closed. Push the lining down inside the bag and press the top edge. Sew the button to the front of the bag at the center near the top edge.

kids' bags

ticking tote

This cheerful and roomy tote bag would look great in a child's room, but it has a broad-enough appeal to make it useful for adults, too. If you don't have ticking, you could use some other sturdy decorator fabric, such as old curtains. The central motif, cut from a tea towel, gives it extra pizzazz.

1 Turn under and press ⅝in (1.5cm) on the side and bottom edges of the pocket. On the top edge, turn under and press ¼in (5mm) and then ¾in (2cm); topstitch this hem across the top. Place the pocket, right side up, on the right side of the front/back, 4in (10cm) in from the right-hand edge and centered between the top and bottom edges. Pin in place, baste, and then topstitch around the side and bottom edges and down the middle from top to bottom. Using a contrasting thread, zigzag stitch small bands of stitches at the top corners and in the center.

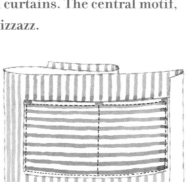
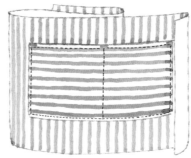

MATERIALS

1 piece of ticking (cut with stripes horizontal), 14¼ x 7¾in (36 x 19.5cm), for pocket

1 piece of ticking (cut with stripes vertical), 44¼ x 13in (112 x 33cm), for front/back

1 piece of ticking (cut with stripes horizontal), 44¼ x 11½in (112 x 29cm), for band

1 piece of ticking and 1 piece of thick plastic, each 17 x11in (42 x 28cm), for base

2 pieces of ticking (cut with stripes horizontal), each 5½ x 32in (14 x 81cm), for handles

1 piece of contrasting fabric, 6 x 3¾in (15 x 9.5cm), for central motif

Matching and contrasting sewing thread

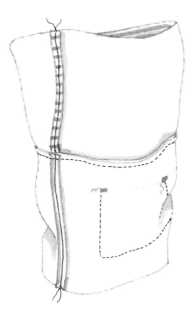

2 With right sides together, pin the two short edges of the front/back together with a ⅝in (1.5cm) side seam. To check that the front/back will fit the base exactly, use the template on page 125 to cut out the oval base from the ticking. Pin the lower edge of the front/back temporarily to the base, right sides together, with a ⅝in (1.5cm) seam. Adjust the width of the side seam if necessary, unpin the base, and stitch the side seam. Pin the short edges of the band with right sides together, and stitch a seam of the same width as the side seam. Press both seams open and zigzag stitch the seam allowances. With right sides together, pin the bottom edge of the band to the top edge of the front/back, aligning the side seams. Stitch a ⅝in (1.5cm) seam. Press the seam allowances toward the band, and open out the band as shown.

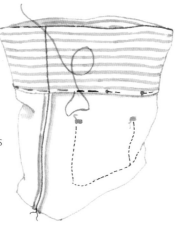

3 On the top edge of the band, turn under and press ⅝in (1.5cm). Now fold the band in half, wrong sides together, and pin the turned-under edge over the seam you've just stitched in step 2, covering the seam allowance. Baste.

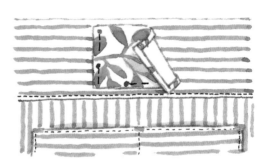

4 Topstitch the band in place from the right side of the bag, close to the edge. Turn under and press ¼in (5mm) on all four edges of the contrasting fabric. Pin and baste this to the band at center front. Topstitch all four edges of the motif.

5 Fold one handle in half lengthwise, right sides together. Pin and stitch a ¼in (5mm) seam down the side and across one end. Turn right side out and turn in ¼in (5mm) at the open end; baste the end. Repeat for the other handle. Pin the ends of one handle to the front band, 1¾in (4.5cm) from the sides, and with the bottom edges even with the bottom edge of the band. Topstitch as shown. Attach the other handle to the band back in the same way.

6 Cut out the plastic to match the ticking base. Pin the plastic to the wrong side of the ticking, and baste around the edges. With the bag wrong side out, pin the base to the lower edge of the bag, with right sides together and raw edges even. Pin, baste, and stitch a ⅝in (1.5cm) seam all around the base; zigzag stitch the seam allowances. Turn the bag right side out, press, and remove basting.

label bag

When making bags I use a lot of old items of clothing, and I always keep the labels from them. Sewn together, they make a unique and eye-catching patchwork, with an attractive mix of styles and color contrasts. This patchwork is definitely a labor of love, so you may prefer to use the technique when making one of the smaller purses in this book. For the handles I used some ribbon salvaged from wrapping, while the back and the lining are made from portions of shirts. The shirt section I used had little button loops, so I incorporated them and a button band, but you could just as easily use a buttonhole band instead of the loops.

MATERIALS

1 piece of shirt fabric, 9 x 9in (23 x 23cm), with button-loop or buttonhole band on one edge, for lining front

1 piece of shirt fabric, 9 x 9in (23 x 23cm), with button band on one edge, for lining back

1 piece of shirt fabric, 9 x 9⅜in (23 x 24cm), for back

Selection of fabric labels, for front

1 ribbon, 55in (140cm) long

Matching sewing thread

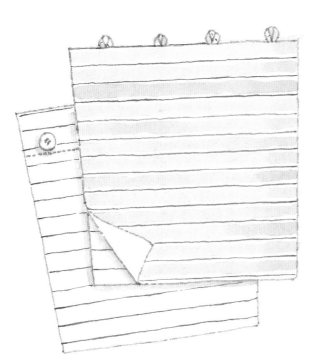

1 With the button band on the top edge, taper the sides of the lining pieces so they are each 9in (23cm) wide at the top and 8in (20.5cm) wide at the bottom, with a depth of 9in (23cm). Lay the back piece (with the button-loop band on the top edge) under one of these, aligning the bottom edges, and trim the sides of the back piece to match the lining.

2 For the front, lay out the labels on a flat surface and arrange them like a jigsaw, until the area they cover is as large as the lining. Make sure the top edge is straight. You will need to turn under and press about ⅛in (3mm) on any raw edges (apart from any that will be on the side or bottom edges of the bag front). Sew adjacent labels together by placing them with right sides together, and hand sewing the edges together using overhand stitch as shown. Open the labels out flat after sewing. When complete, press the front.

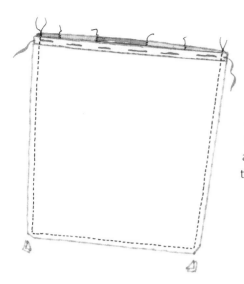

3 Turn under and press ⅜in (1cm) along the top edge of the back piece; baste. With right sides together, pin the front to the back around the side and bottom edges. Stitch a ⅜in (1cm) seam, pivoting at the corners. Press. Trim the front to match the back, and snip off the corners of the seam allowances. Place the lining front and back with right sides together; pin and stitch in the same way.

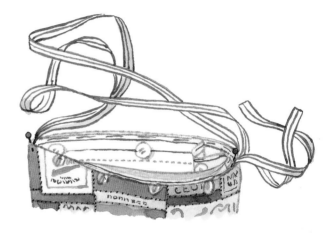

4 With the main fabric right side out and the lining wrong side out, put the lining inside the main fabric so that wrong sides are together. Fold the ribbon in half, and pin the folded end to the bag top edge at one corner, sandwiching it between the main fabric and the lining. Measure 5½in (14cm) from the loose ends of the ribbon, and at this point sew both halves of the ribbon to the outside of the bag. Pin the lining to the main fabric around the top edge; topstitch close to the edge. Remove the basting and press the bag. Tie the loose ends of the ribbon into a bow at the side.

beanie hat purse

This charming wooly purse is made from a beanie hat that has been felted, while the attached bird is made from a fleecy glove that had lost its mate. Neatly closing the top is a recycled zipper—recycling is a great way to give a new lease on life to items languishing at the back of a cupboard.

MATERIALS

1 felted wool beanie hat, or felted wool from a sweater (see page 116)

2 pieces of lining fabric, each about 8 x 7in (20.5 x 18cm)

1 zipper, about 6in (15cm) long

1 side-seam label (see page 121)

1 piece of fleece, about 6 x 6in (15 x 15cm), for bird

1 scrap of contrasting fabric, for bird's wings

Embroidery floss in color of your choice

Fiberfill or cut-up pantyhose for bird's stuffing

1 small piece of cord or ribbon

Matching sewing thread

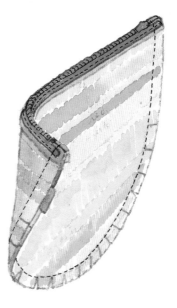

1 Cut the felt into two roughly half-oval shapes for the front and back, each about 7¼in (18cm) wide and 6¼in (16cm) deep. Cut the two pieces of lining to match these. With right sides together, pin the felt front to the felt back along the straight edge; machine baste a ⅝in (1.5cm) seam. Press the seam flat and open out the pieces, forming an oval. Center the closed zipper face down over the basted seam on the wrong side; pin and hand baste the zipper in place near the edges of the zipper tape. With the pieces right side up and the zipper foot on the machine, topstitch down both sides of the zipper about ¼in (5mm) from the seam. Remove all the basting.

2 With right sides together and raw edges even, pin the front to the back around the curved edge. Insert a label in the pinned seam, pointing inward. Stitch a ⅝in (1.5cm) seam, stitching over the ends of the zipper tape (being careful to avoid the zipper stops). Clip into the seam allowances on the curve and trim off the ends of the zipper tape outside the stitching.

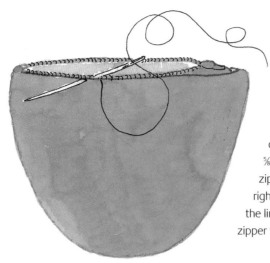

3 Pin the lining front to the lining back around the curved edge with right sides together. Stitch a ⅝in (1.5cm) seam. Clip into the seam allowances on the curve, and press open the seam. Turn under and press ⅝in (1.5cm) along the two straight edges. Open the zipper and, with the felt wrong side out and the lining right side out, put the felt inside the lining, and slipstitch the lining to the felt along the top, keeping it beneath the zipper teeth. Turn right side out.

4 Using the templates on page 125, cut out two pieces for the bird front and back from the fleece, and two wings from the contrasting fabric. Sew a wing to the right side of the front and back, and embroider a French knot for each eye.

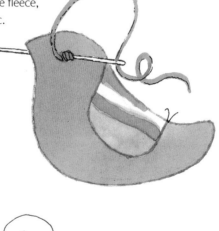

5 Pin the bird front to the bird back with right sides together. Insert a small piece of cord or ribbon in the seam at the top; the longer part of the cord should be on the inside. Stitch a ¼in (5mm) seam all around, leaving a gap in the base. Turn right side out, and stuff with fiberfill or cut-up pieces of pantyhose. Turn in the edges of the opening, pin, and slipstitch it closed. Push the free end of the cord or ribbon between the slipstitches at the top of the purse, and hand sew a few stitches to secure it.

owl pocket bag

This bag takes a little longer to make than some of the simpler styles in this book, but your effort will be rewarded and the bag will be a great favorite with any child. I used a section of an old blanket for the bag itself, although a woolen sweater that you have felted would work just as well. The owl and the appliquéd tree and leaves were made from scraps of old clothes and a glove.

MATERIALS

1 piece cut from a green knitted sweater, 9½ x 6in (24 x 15cm), for owl front and back and for leaves

1 piece of patterned fabric, 4 x 8in (10 x 20cm), for owl wings

1 scrap of white felt for owl outer eyes

1 scrap of orange felt for owl beak and inner eyes and for leaves

Pink yarn or embroidery floss for owl ear-tufts and eye embroidery

Fiberfill or cut-up pantyhose for owl stuffing

2 pieces cut from blanket and 2 pieces of cotton, each 15 x 12in (38 x 30cm), for front and back

1 piece of gray felted wool, 10¼ x 11in (26 x 28cm), for tree

1 piece of gray felted wool, 5 x 7¼in (12.5 x 18cm), for inner pocket

1 side-seam label (see page 121)

2 pieces cut from blanket and 2 pieces of cotton, each 2¼ x 17in (6 x 44cm), for handles

Matching sewing thread

1 Using the templates on page 126, cut out one owl front and one owl back from the green knit, four wings from the patterned fabric, two outer eyes from the white felt, and two inner eyes and a beak from the orange felt. With right sides together, pin a wing to one side of the owl front. Baste and stitch a ¼in (5mm) seam. Repeat for the other wing, and then for the two wings on the owl back. Press the seams away from the wings. Pin and slipstitch the inner eyes to the outer eyes, and then the outer eyes and beak to the owl front. With an embroidery needle and the yarn or floss, embroider the eyes with eyelet stitch (straight stitches radiating out from the center of each eye), bringing the needle up through the middle of the eye each time.

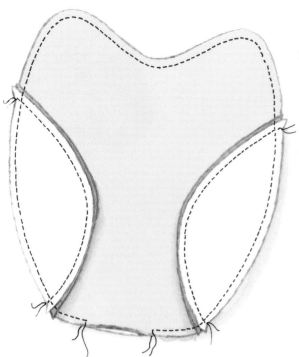

2 Pin the owl front to the owl back with right sides together, and stitch a ¼in (5mm) seam around the edge, leaving an opening at the bottom. Turn right side out and stuff with fiberfill or cut-up pieces of pantyhose. Turn in the edges of the opening, pin, and slipstitch it closed.

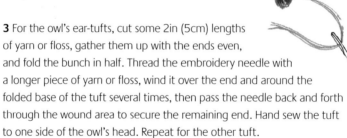

3 For the owl's ear-tufts, cut some 2in (5cm) lengths of yarn or floss, gather them up with the ends even, and fold the bunch in half. Thread the embroidery needle with a longer piece of yarn or floss, wind it over the end and around the folded base of the tuft several times, then pass the needle back and forth through the wound area to secure the remaining end. Hand sew the tuft to one side of the owl's head. Repeat for the other tuft.

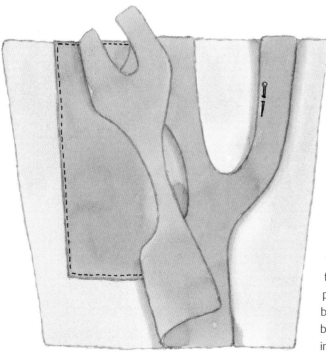

4 Taper the sides of the front and back pieces cut from the blanket and the lining front and back pieces so they each measure 15in (38cm) wide at the top and 10¾in (27.5cm) wide at the bottom, with a depth of 11¾in (30cm). Using the template on page 126, cut out a tree from the gray wool. Place the tree, right side up, on the right side of the bag front, and position the inner pocket between the tree and the bag front so it is centered behind the hole. Remove the tree, then pin and topstitch close to all four edges of the inner pocket. Replace the tree, pin, and baste in place, turning under ¼in (5mm) as you go. On tight curves, clip into this seam allowance before turning under. Topstitch close to all edges of the tree. Using the template on page 126, cut out some leaves from the piece of green sweater and the orange felt. Pin in place, and slipstitch or topstitch to the bag. Complete the bag as for the Mini Bucket Bag on pages 108–11, steps 2–6, but leaving a larger opening in the bottom seam of the lining in step 2. Place the owl in the pocket.

variation

For this project an owl was used, but you can make a whole variety of animals by just choosing some different-colored fabrics and adding other kinds of embellishments. Sew some string whiskers and cut an ellipse shape out of fabric for the pupils on the eyes to create a cat. For a robin use some brown fabric and then cut out a red circle and fix it onto the bottom of the bird for its red breast.

mini bucket bag

With these cute mini bucket bags you can extend the life of all those pretty floral dresses, little check shirts, and favorite tops that the children have grown out of. They look adorable hanging in a row on pegs, to store all those small things that clutter up a child's bedroom. What's more, they are quick and easy to make. Choose fabrics for the linings that provide colorful contrasts with the main fabrics.

MATERIALS (FOR ONE BAG)

2 pieces of main fabric and 2 pieces of lining fabric, each 10½ x 8¼in (27 x 21cm), for front and bag

1 flat or side-seam label (see page 121)

2 pieces of main fabric and 2 pieces of lining fabric, each 2¼ x 12in (6 x 31cm), for handles

1 piece of embroidery floss or fine cord, about 2½in (6.5cm) long, for button loop (optional)

1 button (optional)

Matching sewing thread

1 Taper the main-fabric and lining front and back pieces so that each is 10½in (27cm) wide at the top and 5¼in (13.5cm) wide at the bottom, with a depth of 8¼in (21cm). If you are using a flat label, pin and then topstitch it in position at center front.

2 With right sides together, pin the main-fabric front and back together at the side and bottom edges. If you are using a side-seam label, insert it in the seam, pointing inward; pin. Stitch a ⅝in (1.5cm) seam down the sides and across the bottom, pivoting at the corners. Snip off the corners of the seam allowances and press the seam. Repeat for the lining front and back, but leave a 2¼in (6cm) opening in the seam at the bottom.

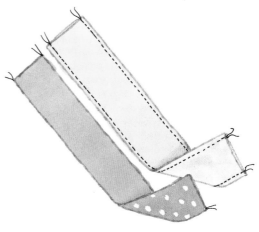

3 Pin a handle piece from the main fabric to one of the handle lining pieces, right sides together. Stitch a ¼in (5mm) seam down each long edge. Repeat for the second handle. Turn the handles right side out and press.

kids' bags

4 With raw edges even, pin the ends of one handle to the right side of the front, 1½in (4cm) from the side edges, and with the handle lining facing inward; baste. Pin and baste the other handle to the back in the same way. If you are incorporating a button loop, pin it in place as shown on page 120 (top left).

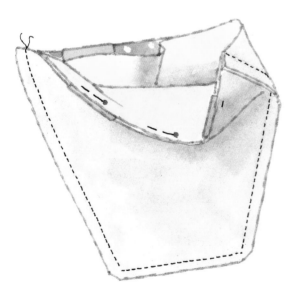

5 With the lining right side out and the main fabric wrong side out, put the lining inside the main fabric, so they are right sides together. Pin the lining to the main fabric all the way around the top, and then stitch a ⅝in (1.5cm) seam, stitching over the ends of the handles (and the loop, if using).

6 Turn the bag right side out through the opening in the bottom of the lining. Turn in the raw edges of the opening, pin, and slipstitch it closed. Push the lining inside the bag. If you are using a button, sew it on at center front.

blue denim button bag

This fun blue denim bag, decorated with large, colorful badges and covered buttons, would make a great present for an older child or teenager. They could add their own badges and cover some buttons with fabric of their choice. The bag has a long strap to allow it to be slung across the body, and so a larger version of it would make a good school bag.

MATERIALS

1 piece of patterned fabric, 12 x 13¾in (30 x 35cm), for flap

1 piece of denim, 9 x 11½in (22 x 29cm), for flap

1 piece of plain fabric, 10¾ x 12¼in (27 x 31.5cm), for front

1 piece of patterned fabric, 10¾ x 13¼in (27 x 33.5cm), for back

1 side-seam label (see page 121)

2 pieces of fabric, each 10¾ x 12¾in (27 x 32.5cm), for lining

1 piece of denim, 1¾ x 39in (4.5 x 100cm), for strap

Selection of colorful fabric scraps, to cover buttons

Covered-button kits

Matching sewing thread

Badges (optional)

1 Turn under and press 1¼in (3cm) on the two long edges of the patterned flap piece. Turn under and press ¾in (2cm) and then a further 1¼in (3cm) along one short edge. (It will become the bottom edge of the flap but is shown in these steps at the top.) This piece should now measure 9½ x 11¾in (24 x 30cm). Slipstitch the double hem at the corners.

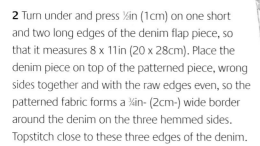

2 Turn under and press ½in (1cm) on one short and two long edges of the denim flap piece, so that it measures 8 x 11in (20 x 28cm). Place the denim piece on top of the patterned piece, wrong sides together and with the raw edges even, so the patterned fabric forms a ¾in- (2cm-) wide border around the denim on the three hemmed sides. Topstitch close to these three edges of the denim.

3 With right sides together, pin the front to the back at the bottom edge. Stitch a ⅝in (1.5cm) seam; press open. Now pin the front to the back at the side edges, with right sides together and the top edges even, so the seam you have just stitched is ½in (1cm) above the fold at the bottom edge. Insert a label, pointing inward, in one side seam, near the top edge; pin. Stitch ⅝in (1.5cm) side seams.

Snip off the corners of the seam allowances and press the seams. Place the two lining pieces with right sides together, and pin along the side and bottom edges. Stitch a ⅝in (1.5cm) seam around the three edges, pivoting at the corners. Snip off the corners of the seam allowances at the bottom. Turn under and press ⅝in (1.5cm) on the top edges of both the main fabric and the lining.

4 For the strap, fray one long edge of the strap piece by using a pin to tease out and remove, one at a time, the lengthwise threads in the fabric to a depth of ⅛–¼in (3–5mm). Turn under and press the other long edge by one third of the width of the unfrayed part of the strip. Now turn under and press the same amount again, so that the strap is three layers thick. Topstitch along the length of the strap, close to the frayed edge.

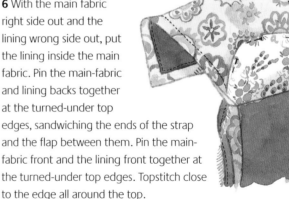

5 Pin the ends of the strap to the wrong side of the main-fabric back, at each side of the turned-under top edge, with the ends overlapping the back by ⅝in (1.5cm). The fringe should be on the outside. Now place the flap on top of the ends of the strap, denim side down, with the raw edge overlapping the turned-under top edge of the back by ⅝in (1.5cm). Pin and baste through the ends of the strap, the flap, and the main-fabric back.

6 With the main fabric right side out and the lining wrong side out, put the lining inside the main fabric. Pin the main-fabric and lining backs together at the turned-under top edges, sandwiching the ends of the strap and the flap between them. Pin the main-fabric front and the lining front together at the turned-under top edges. Topstitch close to the edge all around the top.

7 Remove any visible basting. Cover the buttons (see page 119) and hand sew them to the flap. Add badges if you wish.

variation

This clever project has an added surprise once you have finished putting it
together—it really is two bags in one! If you turn the bag inside out you will
discover that it is fully reversible, so choose carefully when selecting a fabric
for the lining and you will have another gorgeous bag to add to your collection.
You could add some appliqué or rickrack to the inside of the bag to make it
even more special.

techniques

The whole ethos of this book is to make exciting projects out of what you already have, and so the equipment and techniques are as simple as the materials.

Equipment

You need very little equipment to make the projects in this book. A sewing machine is essential, but it can be a very basic model. In addition, you'll need the following:

* A steam iron and ironing board
* Dressmaker's shears for cutting out fabric
* Small, pointy scissors for cutting threads, clipping seam allowances, and trimming
* A flexible measuring tape
* A fabric marker that either fades away after a couple of days or can be brushed off
* Pins and hand-sewing needles (sizes 6–8 are a useful medium size)
* Embroidery needles
* A long ruler and a pencil

Thread and embroidery floss/yarn

Apart from fabric and notions such as zippers and buttons (see page 9), the other essential is sewing thread. Ideally, use synthetic thread for synthetic fabric, cotton thread for cotton fabrics, and silk thread for silk fabrics. If possible, match the colors closely.

For embroidery, you can use whatever you have on hand, but if you want to buy any, here are the main ones you can choose from:

* Stranded embroidery floss (if you wish, you can separate the six strands and use them singly, in pairs, or in threes)
* Brilliant or matte embroidery thread or pearl cotton
* Embroidery yarns such as crewel, Persian, or tapestry yarn

Felted wool

Old sweaters make great purses, especially if they are felted. (Felting is when the wool fibers have shrunk and fused together.) It is ideal for making corsages to embellish bags (see page 16). The edges won't fray, so there is no need for hems. If you want to felt some fabric yourself, first make sure that it is 100 percent wool; it won't felt if it contains any manmade fibers. Put the wool items in the washing machine and wash them on the highest setting. They will emerge shrunken but with that lovely felted look. I sometimes even do this twice for a really felted piece.

IMPORTANT

Dimensions always show the width first. Don't mix your measurements—use either inches or metric, but not both, because the equivalents given are not always exact.

Cutting out

The instructions in this book are mainly based on rectangles. Cut out the pieces to the dimensions specified, using either non-metric measurements or metric measurements (shown in parentheses). Never use the two measurement systems interchangeably, because the equivalents are only approximate. The width is always shown first in this book. Be sure to place the pieces so that the grain runs either lengthwise or crosswise on the rectangles.

If a piece is wider at the top edge than at the bottom edge, or vice versa, and the sides are not curved, the list of materials specifies rectangles using the larger dimension, and then the step-by-step instructions tell you to taper the sides. This is easy—you just mark the dimensions at the top and bottom

edges, making sure that the centers are lined up, and then draw straight lines between the edges.

If the shape is curved, then a template is used to convert the rectangle into the exact shape. The templates are all at the back of the book. Trace or photocopy the relevant one (enlarging it if necessary— see page 122), cut it out, pin this pattern to the fabric, and then cut out the fabric around the pattern.

Interfacing

Some bags will need interfacing, depending on the design and on the fabric, to give body or structure. I have sometimes specified interfacing in a project, but there will probably be other times you will want to use it, when you have chosen thin fabric. In this book I have tried to use recycled fabric as interfacing, which is basted to the main fabric just inside the seamline. Or you can buy it in different weights and in either sew-on or iron-on versions. I use a medium-weight iron-on type if I am not using recycled fabric as interfacing. For the iron-on type, follow the manufacturer's instructions. Once you have basted or ironed the interfacing to the fabric, just treat the piece as one layer.

After stitching seams, either remove the basting or, for the iron-on type, carefully pull the interfacing away from the main fabric within the seam allowance. Trim away the seam allowance of the interfacing close to the seam, to prevent the seams from being too bulky.

Machine stitching

The key to successful machine stitching is stitching slowly and in a straight line. Learn to control the speed so that the machine doesn't run away with you!

Straight machine stitch is used for seams (with a stitch length of 10–12 on a scale of 1–20, and a stitch width of 0).

Topstitching is a straight stitch that is stitched from the right side of the fabric. Because it will be visible when the bag is completed, it's important to stitch in a straight line. For the bags in this book the topstitching should be about ⅛in (3mm) from the edge.

Zigzag stitching is used for finishing seam allowances to stop them from fraying (but this isn't necessary if the bag is lined) and to create a satin-stitch effect in machine embroidery; the stitch width varies according to the fabric and the desired effect.

Basting

This is a temporary way of holding two or more pieces of fabric together before stitching, if pins would get in the way. It's useful when making seams in awkward corners, or when sewing curved edges together, or when another layer will be added on top and you wouldn't be able to get at the pins. Sew long running stitches (see page 120) and don't secure the thread at the end; when you want to remove the basting, just snip off the knot at the start of the thread, and pull the other end. Machine basting is faster than hand basting, and is used to hold a seam together temporarily when inserting a zipper (see page 101), but it is not as useful for intricate work as hand basting.

Stitching seams

Here is how to stitch the plain seams used in this book.

1 Place two pieces of fabric together so their right sides are facing each other and the raw edges are even. Pin the seam, placing the pins either at right angles to the seamline or along the seamline. (To make the stitching line obvious, the illustrations in this book often show the pins along the seamline, but they will have to be removed as you

stitch up to them. In fact, it's a good idea to remove any pins at right angles, too, unless your machine is very good at stitching over them.) If the fabric is thick or the seam is curved, the pins will need to be closer together than on a straight seam on thin fabric.

2 The majority of seams used in this book are the same as seamstresses use—⅝in (1.5cm)—as this gives a strong seam without being too bulky. Sometimes, however, the seams have to be ⅜in (1cm) or ¼in (5mm) wide. The width of the seam is always specified. The "seam allowance" is the fabric between the seamline and the raw edge; in other words, it is as wide as the seam.

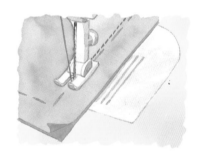

3 ▲ If necessary, baste the seam close to the seamline, just within the seam allowance, and then remove the pins. With the raw edges on the right, stitch a seam of the correct width. To keep the stitching straight, use the stitching guide or a piece of tape the correct distance from the needle.

4 At the beginning and end of each seam, do a few stitches in reverse to secure the thread. When stitching around curves, work slowly so that the curve will be continuous and gradual, and you won't stray off the seamline. It helps to use a slightly shorter stitch length on curves.

5 When you come to a corner, stop ⅝in (1.5cm) from the edge, or whatever the width of the seam is. With the needle at its lowest point, raise the presser foot and pivot the fabric around until the new seamline is in line with the presser foot.

Lower the presser foot and continue stitching along the new seamline. ▼

Trimming and pressing seams

Seams need to be trimmed and pressed to make them lie flat.

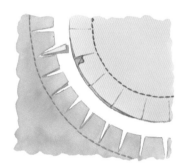

1 ▲ On curved seams, clip into the seam allowance after stitching. For inward curves, the clips should be wedge-shaped notches. For outward curves, they just need to be slits.

2 ▲ On a point, trim away the seam allowances around the point. On square corners, snip off the corners of the seam allowances.

3 When a straight piece of fabric is stitched to a corner of another piece, clip into the seam allowance of the straight piece at the corner. This clip will open up and allow the edges to align with the edges either side of the corner on the other piece. Be careful not to snip beyond the seamline. ▼

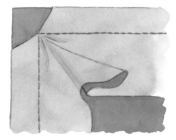

4 ▲ Unless instructed to press a seam toward one side, press it open from the wrong side. Try not to press seams from the right side, as you may mark the fabric. If stitching together two pieces that already have seams, you need to press open the first seams, snip off the corners of the seam allowances, and then align the seams exactly (if appropriate) when pinning the fabric pieces together for the new seam. While stitching the new seam, be careful to keep the seam allowances of the old seams flat.

Gathering

When two pieces of fabric of different widths are stitched together, the wider piece can be gathered, making it the same width as the other piece.

1 On the wider piece, make two rows of hand or machine basting within the seam allowance; at one side secure the ends but at the other side leave long ends rather than securing them. With right sides together, pin the wider piece to the other one at the sides.

2 Carefully pull the two unsecured ends of the hand basting, or the two unsecured bobbin threads of the machine basting. As the fabric gathers

up, gently slide it along the threads. Continue until the wider piece is the same width as the other. Distribute the gathers evenly and pin the two pieces together, spacing the pins closely. ▼

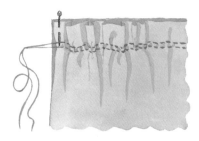

3 Stitch the seam with the gathered piece on top, so that you can make sure the gathers are straight and even.

Lining

If a bag is lined, the lining is usually made in the same way and to the same size as the bag itself. Depending on the style of the bag, it is attached to the bag at the top in one of two ways, which is always explained in the instructions for each bag.

For the first method, the right-side-out lining is placed inside the wrong-side-out bag so the right sides are together. With this method, any label, button loop, or handles are inserted in the seam so that they point inward. After the seam is stitched, the whole bag is turned right side out through the opening in the bottom of the lining. The edges of the opening are turned in, pinned, and slipstitched.

For the second method, the lining doesn't need an opening in the bottom. The top edges of the bag and the lining are turned under and pressed. The wrong-side-out lining is placed inside the right-side-out bag so the wrong sides are together. With this method, any label, button loop, or handles are inserted in the seam so that they point outward. The lining is either topstitched or slipstitched to the bag around the top (but if there are handles, slipstitching would not be strong enough to hold them in place, so topstitching must be used).

Handles

These can be made in several different ways. In each case, the ends are finished if they will be visible on the completed bag, or left unfinished if they will be inserted in a seam.

▲ **An invisible-stitching handle** is neat because you can't see any stitching, but the fabric cannot be too bulky or the handle too narrow. Fold the handle piece in half lengthwise with right sides together. Pin and stitch a ¼in (5mm) seam down the long edge and across one end, forming a fabric tube. Press the seam. To turn it right side out, place the stitched end over the blunt end of a skewer or knitting needle and pull the fabric tube down over it. Once you can see the end emerging, pull it the rest of the way. Press. If the ends of the handle will show, turn in ¼in (5mm) on the open end and slipstitch the opening closed.

▲ **A topstitched handle** is best when the fabric is bulky or the handle is so narrow that it would be difficult to turn it right side out after stitching the seam. Turn under and press ¼in (5mm) on the long edges (and at the ends if these will be visible on the bag). Fold it in half lengthwise, wrong sides together, and press. Pin and topstitch close to the turned-under edges. When attaching the handle, place the unstitched edge on the outside.

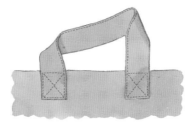

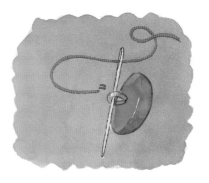

▲ A double-thick topstitched handle is useful if the fabric is thin, as the seam allowances cannot be seen. Fold the long edges in to meet at the center; press. If the ends will be visible on the bag, also fold in ¼in (5mm) at each end. Now fold it in half lengthwise. Pin and topstitch close to the turned-under edges. When attaching the handle, place the unstitched edge on the outside.

▲ To attach handles so the ends are visible, pin the ends to the completed bag (usually on the outside), and topstitch a rectangle (with or without a cross in the middle) at each end.

Buttons

Covered buttons can be made by covering a shank button or by covering a button form from a covered-button kit.

▲ To attach a shank button, make a few backstitches on the right side of the fabric, then make small stitches through the hole in the shank. Secure the thread on the wrong side of the fabric.

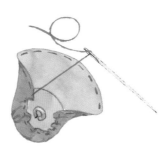

▲ A two-piece handle can be used if you want a different fabric for the top than for the underside. Either turn under and press ¼in (5mm) along the long edges of both pieces (and at the ends if these will be visible), pin one piece to the other with wrong sides together, and topstitch as shown above; or join the pieces with right sides together and then turn right side out.

▲ To cover a shank button, cut a circle of fabric ¼in (5mm) larger than the button all around, i.e. with a diameter ½in (1cm) bigger, or more if it is a thick button. Gather the edge (see page 118). Wrap the circle over the button and secure in place by hand sewing from one side to the other, pulling the gathered fabric tight until the fabric is smooth.

▲ To attach buttons with holes, make a few backstitches on the right side of the fabric, then bring the needle up through one of the holes in the button. Place a pin, toothpick, or matchstick on top of the button (this isn't necessary if the button won't be used and is only decorative). Insert the needle through the opposite hole, taking it down to the wrong side of the fabric. Bring the needle up again through the first hole and back down again through the second hole. Repeat several times. If there are four holes, bring the needle up through one of the other holes, and repeat for that pair of holes. (You can, if you prefer, make the stitches through diagonally opposite pairs of holes.) To finish, take the needle down through a hole but not through the fabric, remove the pin, toothpick, or matchstick, raise the button, and wrap the thread several times around the thread shank that you have created under the button. Secure the thread with a few small stitches into this shank.

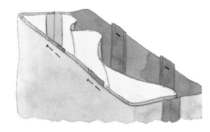

▲ To attach handles by inserting in a seam, pin them between two layers (usually the main fabric and the lining) that will be stitched right sides together. The ends should point outward and the handles point inward, so that when the bag is turned right side out, the handles will stick out of the seam.

▲ To cover a button form, cut a circle of fabric that is slightly less than twice the button form's diameter, and gather the edges (see page 118). Wrap the circle over the button-form so that the edges catch on the tiny hooks on the underside of the button form, then press the back plate from the kit into position to cover the raw edges.

Button loops

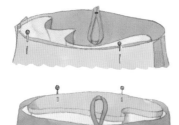

▲ These are made from fabric (see page 36, step 4), ribbon (see page 91, step 2), or twisted cord (see below) and inserted into a seam before the seam is stitched. If it is a seam where the pieces are being stitched right sides together, place the loop so that it is points inward (see above, top illustration)—this will make it stick out from the seam when the fabric is turned right side out. If the seam is formed from two turned-under edges being topstitched with wrong sides together, place the loop so it points outward (see above, bottom illustration).

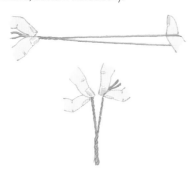

▲ To make a twisted-cord button loop, you'll need to either ask a friend to lend a hand (literally) or use your teeth! Cut a length of embroidery floss or yarn four times the desired length of the finished cord. Fold it in half and hold the two ends in your left hand. Insert the index finger of your right hand in the loop at the other end and circle your hand around and around until the floss or yarn has twisted tightly against your finger. Ask your friend to hold the middle (or grab it with your teeth), and bring your hands still holding the ends together. Your friend, or your teeth, can now let go of the middle, and allow the two halves of the cord to twist around and around each other. Knot the ends.

Hand stitches

The main stitches used for hand sewing in this book are slipstitch, running stitch, and overhand stitch. In addition, basic hand embroidery stitches are used for decoration, in particular running stitch, backstitch, straight stitch, and French knot.

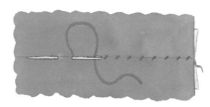

▲ **Slipstitch** is ideal for sewing two folded edges, such as seam allowances, together almost invisibly. Hide the knot inside one fold, bringing the needle out through the fold. Insert it into the other fold 1⁄16in (1–2mm) farther along. Slip the needle along inside that fold, bringing it out 1⁄4in (5mm) farther along. Repeat on the opposite side, continuing to the end.

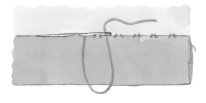

▲ **Slipstitch** can also be used to sew a folded edge to a flat piece. Hide the knot inside the fold, bringing the needle out through the fold. Insert it into the flat piece 1⁄16in (1–2mm) farther along, picking up only a few threads of the fabric. Insert the needle into the folded edge 1⁄16in (1–2mm) farther along. Slip it along inside the fold, bringing it out 1⁄4in (5mm) farther along. Repeat, continuing to the end.

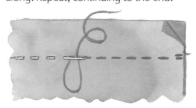

▲ **Running stitch** is used for gathering, hand basting, and hand embroidery. Secure the thread with a couple of small stitches, and then make several stitches by bringing the needle up and back down

through the fabric several times along the stitching line. Pull the needle through and repeat. Try to keep the stitches and spaces the same size. (Sashiko stitch, a decorative variation, is a running stitch in which the spaces between stitches are slightly smaller than the stitches themselves.)

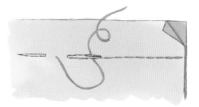

▲ **Backstitch** is used for embroidering a continuous line, as well as for strong hand-stitched seams and for securing the thread at the beginning and end of hand sewing. Working from right to left along the stitching line, bring the needle up from the back, insert it in the fabric one stitch length to the right, and bring it up one stitch length to the left. Insert it at the left-hand end of the previous stitch. Continue in this way to the end.

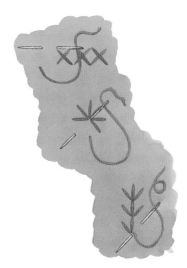

▲ **Straight stitch** is used in different arrangements to form other embroidery stitches, such as **cross stitch** (see above, top illustration), **eyelet stitch** (see above, center illustration), and **fern stitch** (see above, bottom illustration)—all of which involve inserting the needle at the point where the thread has previously come out—as well as other stitches such as satin stitch. I use these a lot on the labels used for the bags (see page 121).

▲ **French knots** also involve inserting the needle at the point where the thread has emerged, but the needle is twisted around the thread twice before it is reinserted (see page 23, step 2).

Labels

These give bags a professional designer look. I have used a variety of labels throughout, some with embroidery motifs and some just contrasting strips of material. Shown here are some of the embroidery motifs you could use. All the labels are either two-sided labels that are inserted into a side seam or are flat labels that are topstitched to fabric.

▲ **For a side-seam label**, cut out a piece of fabric twice the desired width, plus ¼in (5mm), by the desired length, plus ½in (1cm). Embroider the motif on half of it, or on both halves if you prefer, being careful not to embroider within ¼in (5mm) of the edge. Fold the label in half, right sides together. Pin and stitch a ¼in (5mm) seam across the top and bottom. Trim the seam allowances to ⅛in (3mm) and turn right side out. Press. When inserting the label into the side seam

that is being stitched with the fabric pieces right sides together, the raw edges of the label should be pointing outward and the fold inward. When the bag is turned right side out, the label will stick out of the seam.

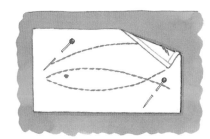

▲ **For a flat label**, cut out a piece of fabric the desired width plus ½in (1cm), by the desired length plus ½in (1cm). Turn under and press ¼in (5mm) on each edge. Embroider the motif, pin the label in position on the right side of the bag fabric, and topstitch in place.

Embroidery motifs

To embroider the motifs shown below, use the following stitches:

Top left group: Eyelet stitch with French knots on the ends and backstitch for the stem if used.

Top right group: French knots and backstitch for the stem if used.

Bottom left group: Fern stitch with French knots on the ends and backstitch for the stem and outline if used.

Bottom right group: Backstitch with French knot for eye.

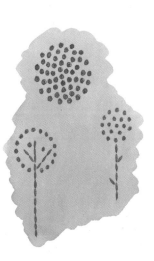

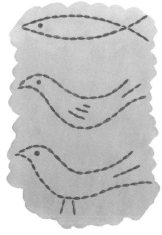

◀▲ **Embroidery motifs for labels**

templates

Some templates overlap on the pages, but you can tell them apart by the color. Photocopy the template, either to the same size (if labeled "actual size") or so that the photocopy is twice the width and twice the height (if labeled "enlarge to twice this size"). Cut out the shape from the photocopy, pin this pattern to your fabric, and cut around it.

If a template has a heavy dotted line saying "place on fold," it is for only half the piece. You need to fold the fabric in half on the straight grain, place that edge of the pattern exactly on the fold, and then pin and cut through both layers (but don't cut along the fold line). When you unfold it, you have the complete piece.

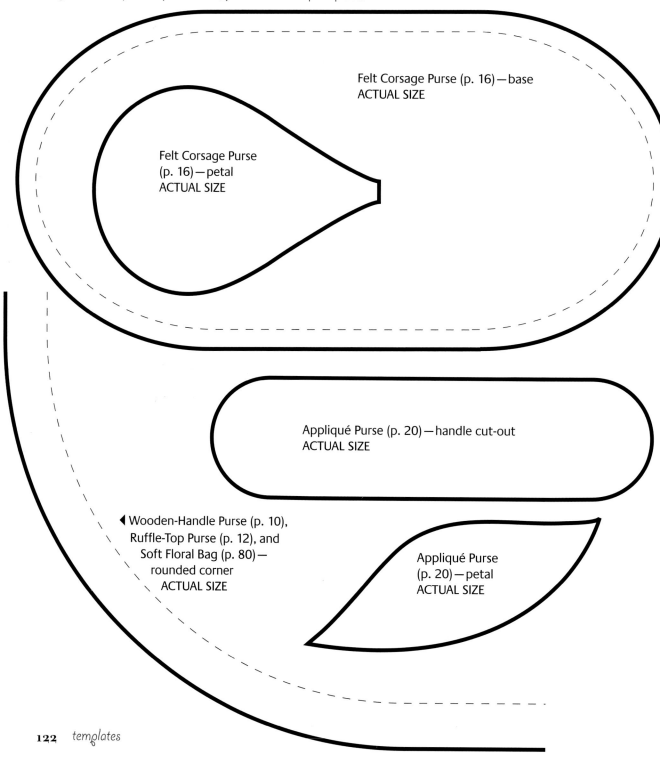

Felt Corsage Purse (p. 16) — base
ACTUAL SIZE

Felt Corsage Purse
(p. 16) — petal
ACTUAL SIZE

Appliqué Purse (p. 20) — handle cut-out
ACTUAL SIZE

◀ Wooden-Handle Purse (p. 10),
Ruffle-Top Purse (p. 12), and
Soft Floral Bag (p. 80) —
rounded corner
ACTUAL SIZE

Appliqué Purse
(p. 20) — petal
ACTUAL SIZE

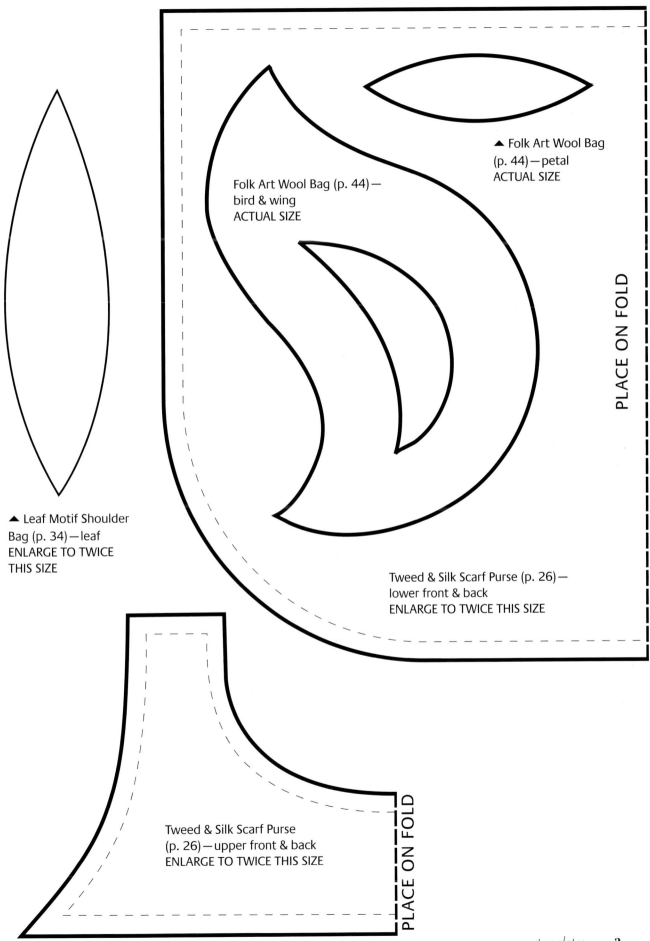

▲ Folk Art Wool Bag
(p. 44)—petal
ACTUAL SIZE

Folk Art Wool Bag (p. 44)—
bird & wing
ACTUAL SIZE

▲ Leaf Motif Shoulder
Bag (p. 34)—leaf
ENLARGE TO TWICE
THIS SIZE

PLACE ON FOLD

Tweed & Silk Scarf Purse (p. 26)—
lower front & back
ENLARGE TO TWICE THIS SIZE

Tweed & Silk Scarf Purse
(p. 26)—upper front & back
ENLARGE TO TWICE THIS SIZE

PLACE ON FOLD

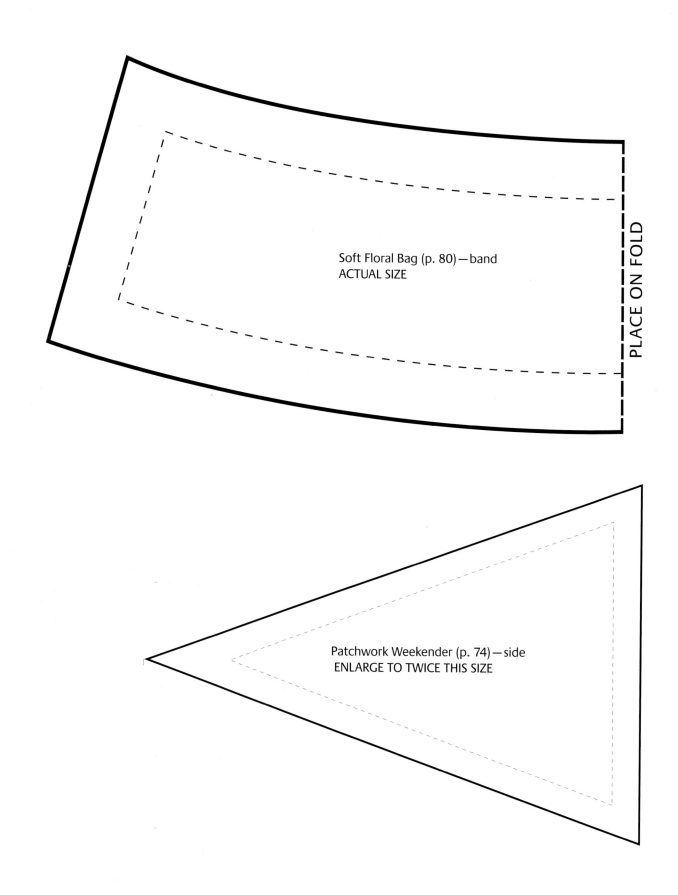

Soft Floral Bag (p. 80) — band
ACTUAL SIZE

PLACE ON FOLD

Patchwork Weekender (p. 74) — side
ENLARGE TO TWICE THIS SIZE

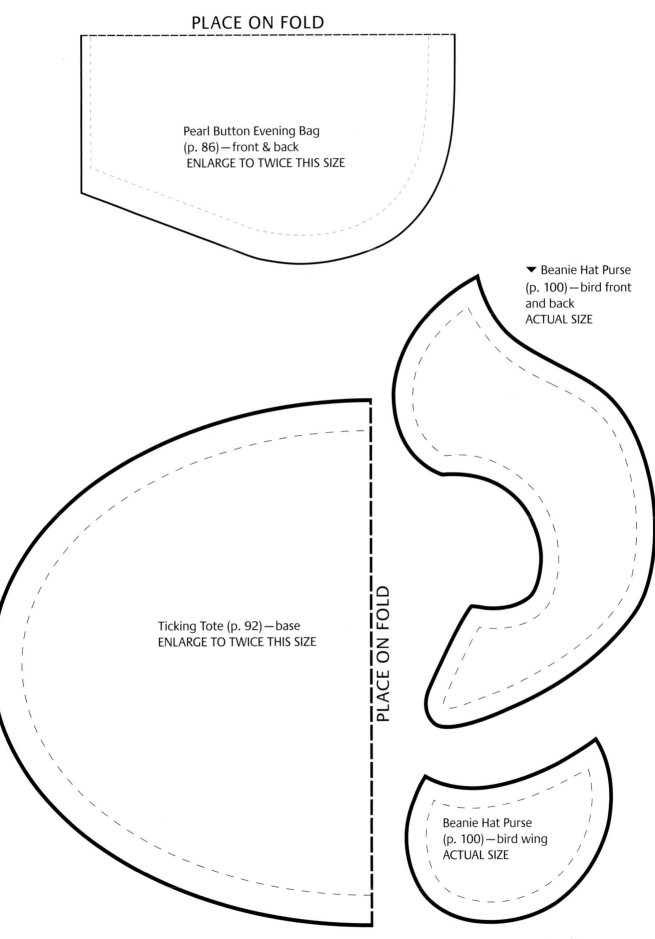

PLACE ON FOLD

Pearl Button Evening Bag
(p. 86)—front & back
ENLARGE TO TWICE THIS SIZE

▼ Beanie Hat Purse
(p. 100)—bird front
and back
ACTUAL SIZE

Ticking Tote (p. 92)—base
ENLARGE TO TWICE THIS SIZE

PLACE ON FOLD

Beanie Hat Purse
(p. 100)—bird wing
ACTUAL SIZE

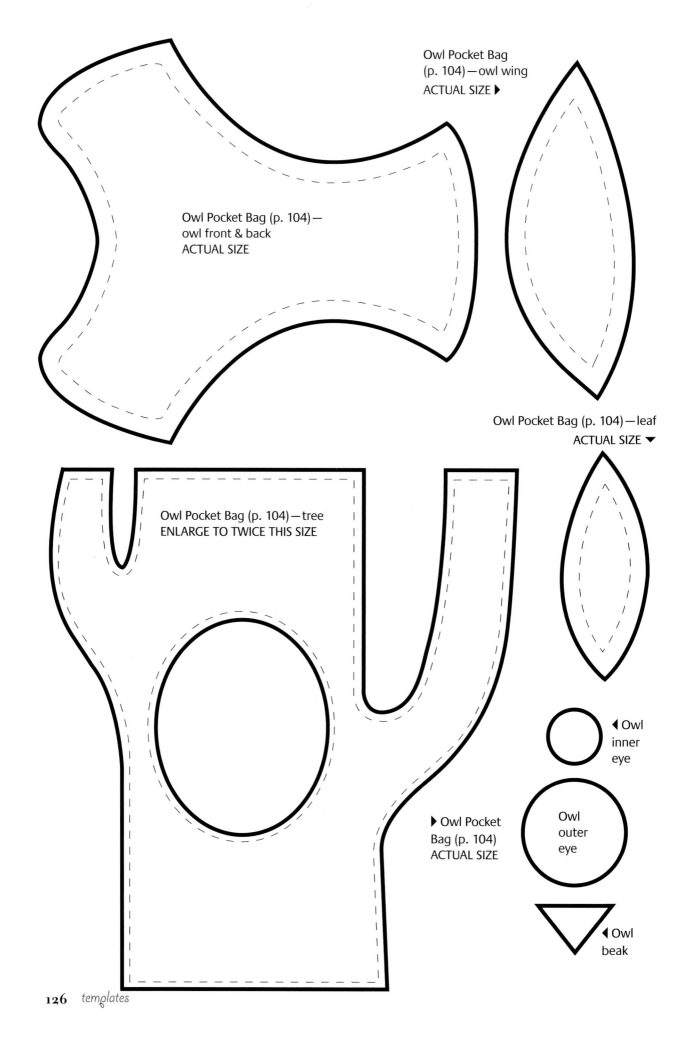

Owl Pocket Bag
(p. 104)—owl wing
ACTUAL SIZE ▶

Owl Pocket Bag (p. 104)—
owl front & back
ACTUAL SIZE

Owl Pocket Bag (p. 104)—leaf
ACTUAL SIZE ▼

Owl Pocket Bag (p. 104)—tree
ENLARGE TO TWICE THIS SIZE

◀ Owl
inner
eye

▶ Owl Pocket
Bag (p. 104)
ACTUAL SIZE

Owl
outer
eye

◀ Owl
beak

suppliers

U.S. STOCKISTS

Amy Butler
www.amybutler.com

B. B. Bargoons
8201 Keele Street
Concord, ON L4K 1Z4
1-800-665-9227
www.bbbargoons.com

Britex Fabrics
146 Geary Street
San Francisco, CA 94108
415-392-2910
www.britexfabrics.com

Buy Fabrics
8967 Rand Avenue
Daphne, Al 36526
877-625-2889
www.buyfabrics.com

Cia's Palette
4155 Grand Avenue S
Minneapolis, MN 55409
612-229-5227
www.ciaspalette.com

Denver Fabrics
10490 Baur Blvd. St.
St. Louis, MO 63132
1-800-468-0602

Discount Fabrics USA
108 N. Carroll Street.
Thurmont, MD 21788
301-271-2266
www.discountfabricsusacorp.com

DoxieShop.com
www.doxieshop.com

FabDir.com
The Internet's largest fabric
store directory
www.fabdir.com

Fabricland/Fabricville
Over 170 stores in Canada
www.fabricland.com
www.fabricville.com

Hobby Lobby
Stores nationwide
www.hobbylobby.com

J & O Fabrics
9401 Rt. 130
Pennsauken, NJ 08110
856-663-2121
www.jandofabrics.com

Jo-Ann Fabric and Craft Store
Stores nationwide
1-888-739-4120
www.joann.com

Lucy's Fabrics
103 S. College Street
Anna, TX 75409
866-544-5829
www.lucysfabrics.com

Purl Patchwork
147 Sullivan Street
New York, NY 10012
212-420-8798
www.purlsoho.com

Reprodepot Fabrics
413-527-4047
www.reprodepotfabrics.com

Tinsel Trading Company
1 West 37th Street
New York, NY 10018
212-730-1030
www.tinseltrading.com

Vogue Fabrics
718-732 Main Street
Evanston, IL 60202
847-864-9600

Wazoodle
2–9 Heritage Road
Markham, ON L3P 1M3
1-866-473-4628
www.wazoodle.com

Z and S Fabrics
681 S. Muddy Creek Road
Denver, PA 17157
717-336-4026
www.zandsfabrics.com

U.K. STOCKISTS

The Button Queen
76 Marylebone Lane
London W1U 2PR
020 7935 1505
www.thebuttonqueen.co.uk

Cath Kidston
08450 262440
www.cathkidston.co.uk

The Cloth House
47 Berwick Street
London W1F 8SJ
020 7437 5155
www.clothhouse.com

Fabrics Galore
52–54 Lavender Hill
London SW11 5RH
020 7738 9589

Ian Mankin
109 Regent's Park Road
London NW1 8UR
020 7722 0997
www.ianmankin.com

Laura Ashley
0871 230 2301
www.lauraashley.com

John Lewis
Oxford Street
London W1A 1EX
020 7629 7711
www.johnlewis.com

Liberty
Regent Street
London W1B 5AH
020 7734 1234
www.liberty.co.uk

The Quilt Room
20 West Street
Dorking
Surrey RH4 1BL
01306 877307
www.quiltroom.co.uk

Tikki Patchwork
293 Sandycombe Road
Kew Gardens
Surrey TW9 3LU
020 8948 8462
www.tikkilondon.com

VV Rouleaux
102 Marylebone Lane
London W1U 2QD
020 7224 5179
www.vvrouleaux.com

index

acknowledgments

I wish to thank everyone that helped with the making of this book. All at CICO especially Cindy, Pete, Sally, Alison, and Barbara. The photographers Carolyn Barber and Emma Mitchell and the stylists Rose Hammick and Catherine Woram for the wonderful photography and the illustrator Kate Simunek for the illustrations that fit so perfectly with the style of the book.

A huge thank you to Ian for all his encouragement and unending support, and of course thanks to Milly, Florence, Henrietta, and Harvey for their enthusiasm in all that I do and their constructive criticism!